Simple Career Planning for Teens and Young Adults

A College Professor's Five-Step Guide to Finding Direction, College Admission, and Preparing for Your Dream Job

Dr. Bridget Ledford Waters

© **Copyright 2023 - All rights reserved.**

The content contained within this book may not be reproduced, duplicated, or transmitted without direct written permission from the author or the publisher.

Under no circumstances will any blame or legal responsibility be held against the publisher, or author, for any damages, reparation, or monetary loss due to the information contained within this book, either directly or indirectly.

Legal Notice:

This book is copyright protected. It is only for personal use. You cannot amend, distribute, sell, use, quote, or paraphrase any par or the content within this book without the consent of the author or publisher.

Disclaimer Notice:

Please note the information contained within this document is for educational and entertainment purposes only. All effort has been executed to present accurate, up-to-date, reliable, complete information. No warranties of any kind are declared or implied. Readers acknowledge that the author is not engaged in the rendering of legal, financial, medical or professional advice. The content within this book has been derived from various sources. Please consult a licensed professional before attempting any techniques outlined in this book.

By reading this document, the reader agrees that under no circumstances is the author responsible for any losses, direct or indirect, that are incurred as a result of the use of the information contained within this document, including, but not limited to, errors, omissions, or inaccuracies.

Table of Contents

INTRODUCTION 1
   WORDS OF ENCOURAGEMENT 2
CHAPTER 1: DETERMINE YOUR INTERESTS AND PERSONALITY 5
   TOP FOUR PERSONALITY TESTS 6
      Myers-Briggs Type Indicator (MBTI) 7
      16 Personalities 9
      The Big Five Personalities 10
      Type A, B, C, and D Personalities 12
CHAPTER 2: CHOOSE THE CAREER PATH THAT'S RIGHT FOR YOU 17
   COMPARING JOBS WITH PERSONALITIES 18
      The Best Career Choices for Myers-Briggs Type Indicator (MBTI)
      and 16 Personalities Types 19
         INTJ (The Mastermind)-Introverted, Intuitive, Thinking, Judging 19
         INTP (The Logician)-Introverted, Intuitive, Thinking, Perceiving 20
         INFP (The Mediator)-Introverted, Intuitive, Feeling, Perceiving 21
         INFJ (The Sage)-Introverted, Intuitive, Feeling, Judging 22
         ISTP (The Tinkerer)-Introverted, Sensing, Thinking, Perceiving 22
         ISTJ (The Archivist)-Introverted, Sensing, Thinking, Judging 23
         ISFP (The Adventurer)-Introverted, Sensing, Feeling, Perceiving 24
         ISFJ (The Defender)-Introverted, Sensing, Feeling, Judging 25
         ENTJ (The General)-Extroverted, Intuitive, Thinking, Judging 25
         ENTP (The Debater)-Extroverted, Intuitive, Thinking, Perceiving 26
         ENFP (The Optimist)-Extroverted, Intuitive, Feeling, Perceiving 27
         ENFJ (The Guide) - Extroverted, Intuitive, Feeling, Judging 28
         ESTJ (The Administrator)-Extroverted, Sensing, Thinking, Judging 29
         ESTP (The Daredevil)-Extroverted, Sensing, Thinking, Perceiving 30
         ESFJ (The Caregiver)-Extroverted, Sensing, Feeling, Judging 30
         ESFP (The Entertainer)-Extroverted, Sensing, Feeling, Perceiving 31
      The Best Career Choices for Each Big Five Personality Traits 32
         Career Choices for High Openness 33
         Career Choices for High Conscientiousness 33
         Career Choices for High Extroversion 34

Career Choices for High Agreeableness 35
Career Choices for High Neuroticism 35
The Best Career Choices for A, B, C, and D Personality Types 36
Career Choices for Type A Personality 36
Career Choices for Type B Personality 37
Career Choices for Type C Personality 37
Career Choices for Type D Personality 38

CHAPTER 3: GET PERSPECTIVE THROUGH RESEARCH AND ADVICE 39

THINGS TO CONSIDER BEFORE CHOOSING A CAREER 40
Talents, Skills, and Personality 40
Education and Training 41
Your Goals and Purpose 43
Employment Opportunities 45
Work-Life Balance 46

CHAPTER 4: PLAN YOUR PATHWAY 53

PURSUING HIGHER EDUCATION 54
Starting College While in High School 54
Attending Community College or Trade School 58
Attending University 60
Public vs. Private Universities 62
Entering the Military 65
The Difference Between Being Enlisted and Commissioned 69
Does University Prestige Matter? 71
Careers That Do Not Require a Four-Year Degree 73

CHAPTER 5: SOME ROADS ARE LONGER THAN OTHERS 83

ADVANCING TO GRADUATE DEGREES 85
Three Types of Graduate Degrees 86
Careers That Require Graduate Degrees 89
Master's Degree Careers 89
Ph.D. Careers 94
Professional Doctorate Careers 97
Benefits of Getting Graduate Degrees 100

CHAPTER 6: THE COLLEGE STARTING LINE 103

COLLEGE PREPARATION AND APPLICATION 104
Applying for College 105
Get Informed 106
Gather the Necessary Materials 106
Organize Materials 107

Personal Statement Essays 109
Asking for a Letter of Recommendation 109
Reviewing and Submission 110
Applying for Scholarships *110*
Obtaining Financial Aid *113*

CHAPTER 7: CHANGING COURSE AND REACHING THE FINISH LINE ...119

THE MANY PATHS YOU CAN TAKE 120
What to Consider When Changing Your College Major *121*
- Time and Money 121
- Consult with an Academic Counselor 122
- Decide Early 122
- Identify the Benefits of Switching 122

Options to Consider After Graduation *123*

CONCLUSION 129

REFERENCES 133

Introduction

I'm sure you have encountered this question at least once: What do you want to be when you grow up? When you were a kid, this question seemed simple–you would utter whichever profession interested you at the time: a doctor, a police officer, or another publicly visible community member. To a young person, this is a fun way to give visions of how adult life works, but as you grow older, this question seems more challenging and more complex to answer, and you're not alone in these feelings. We all progress through adulthood in different ways, yet one challenge seems universal, choosing the right career.

Did you know that only 27% of college graduates have a job closely related to their major? (Plumer, 2013). I am familiar with this fact since I have encountered many university graduates in my years of college teaching, who choose to return to class, needing more education or technical skills to land their dream job. Although education is helpful to get you through the door into entry-level positions in some careers, there are other essential aspects to consider in choosing a career, such as your ability to adapt to your working environment, how you work with other people, how you solve specific problems, and how you communicate professionally, among other things.

There are many opportunities to choose from when shaping your future, and transitioning from one stage of growing up to another allows you to experience many significant milestones. I'm talking about moving up in school, choosing your path after high school graduation, and the next steps you would need to take for your chosen career, leading to "your dream job." Will you choose further education and consider university? If so, what major is best for your career interests? Perhaps you will pursue a job where you learn what it takes to fulfill your duties as you begin working.

This book will assess your personality traits and interests and which jobs best match you. If you excel in creative works and have a keen imagination, it would be bad advice to tell you to be a financial analyst, a job that requires analytical thinking and less creativity. The same thing could be said if you are a person who works well in a team environment but is forced to work in a solitary environment; it simply doesn't match your personal qualities. So, you need a promising career planning strategy that will identify your unique needs and the actions you need to take to set you on a path to success. I will help you find the answers in this book by providing a guide for creating a roadmap toward your chosen career.

Words of Encouragement

This is an exciting and important journey you're embarking on, and I am glad you have taken the first meaningful step toward building a fulfilling and successful future. Career planning is not just about finding a job or making money; it is also about identifying your interests, passions, and strengths and using them to create a path that aligns with your personal and professional goals. Career planning is about exploring the vast array of options and finding the one that truly resonates with who you are and what you want to achieve in the long run.

While the career planning journey may seem daunting at times, it is also an opportunity to learn, grow, and discover new, exciting things about yourself and the world around you. This is a chance to challenge yourself, push your limits, and reach your dreams with passion and determination.

In this book, we will journey through the process of career planning using five simple steps:

1. Determining your personality type and interests

2. Choosing potential career paths based on your personality

3. Researching to determine the best career for your personal and professional goals

4. Understanding the types of higher education institutions and how they can help you enter specific career fields

5. Navigating the college application process, scholarships, and financial aid

Along the way, I will offer simple guidance, tips, advice, and examples to help you work around any challenges you may encounter. Whether you're a high school student, currently enrolled in college or university, just starting your career planning, or a fresh graduate looking for career opportunities, this book will provide the tools and knowledge needed to make the most suitable career choice. While this book helps you through career planning, it should be only one of many resources you use to help you choose. You should also seek support from family members, academic and career counselors, teachers, and other adults you trust. By the time you reach the end of this book, you will have a plan and feel confident in the next steps you need to take toward your dream job.

Before we start, let me tell you a little about myself. My name is Dr. Bridget Ledford Waters (my students know me as Dr. L). I am a certified medical laboratory scientist with 20 years of experience in the medical laboratory field. I am now a professor specializing in medical laboratory education and student advising. As a first-generation college student, I was confused and often overwhelmed with career planning. This taught me how valuable guidance can be in career or educational decisions. I began my journey in higher education in the U.S. Army Reserves in 2001. I completed an eight-year term of service, including achieving two military-trained specialties, a one-year deployment in service of Operation Enduring Freedom in Afghanistan, and reaching the rank of Sergeant.

The military offered me a unique entry into my career, which we will discuss later in Chapter 4. I continued my education in laboratory medicine following my military service, completing a bachelor's degree in May 2009 and Ph.D. in May 2016. Today, I am a program director and professor, a position that allows me to advise and guide students in their college journey toward a professional career.

I'm writing this book because I notice plenty of university students and even graduates who need clarification about their options when it comes to education and their future employment. I am passionate about spreading knowledge about those opportunities and alleviating roadblocks regarding career and college choices. I want to help you obtain a career that fulfills your expectations because it's essential to enjoy your profession and live a fulfilled life with a job that motivates you daily. With my guidance, I hope you can avoid many of the proverbial "bumps in the road" that many other career seekers often face.

Chapter 1:

Determine Your Interests and Personality

Your personality has a huge role in your chosen career, but some people might overlook this fact. When observing any particular company, you may notice that the accounting team members are usually quiet and reserved. In contrast, the marketing team always seems outgoing and vocal in social situations. Your unique personality might help you quickly adapt to specific jobs. So, when looking for a career, taking a personality test beforehand is a great idea. There are multiple personality tests out there, and it is usually beneficial to take more than one. When your career matches your personality, you are more comfortable daily, and the career outcome will be more rewarding through the years. I suppose you are wondering why you should take multiple personality tests when you can get answers using just one. A personality test can tell a couple of things about you. Still, when you take multiple tests that ask different questions or ask them in different ways, you get a comprehensive idea of your overall personality profile.

Sometimes your personality results may not completely match your full personality type. While rare, this may be the case because tests are designed to generalize certain personality types and categorize them under specific labels. These labels, however, will sometimes only describe parts of who you are accurately. Personality tests may not fully represent a person because, rather than allowing someone to describe themselves in their own words, tests are made up of multiple-choice questions with four possible answers (on average), leading to general categorizations of a person's personality. Once you have the results of the tests, it's essential to analyze them further and determine how accurate they are regarding your complete personality.

This chapter will go over four major personality tests and personality categorization methods. For each test, web addresses and QR codes will allow you to take several tests to get multiple category results for your personality before moving on to chapter two.

Top Four Personality Tests

You might be wondering why it is so important to take personality tests when you're only applying for jobs. Research says that about 76% of organizations rely on personality tests for hiring, which is expected to increase in the upcoming years (Chamorro-Premuzic, 2015). Employers use personality tests for various reasons; for instance, they can determine a candidate's natural strengths and better understand their work style and interactions with co-workers. It's also an effective way to find out what determines which candidate will fit a particular job setting. So, it's essential to delve deeper into your personality type to find the most suitable job position before applying. The tests described in this chapter are an excellent way to determine your type. Being 100% self-aware is challenging, so taking a personality test is the first step toward discovering yourself. Then, you can figure out which kind of career would suit you. Four standard personality tests include the Myers-Briggs Type Indicator (MBTI), 16 Personalities, The Big Five Personalities, and the A, B, C, and D Personalities.

Myers-Briggs Type Indicator (MBTI)

Developed as far back as the 1940s, this is the most widely used personality test, devised by Katharine Cook Briggs and her daughter, Isabel Briggs Myers. This test allows people to describe themselves in four-letter codes (ENTJ, ESFP, etc.) The four key groupings will determine where your personality fits according to polar perspectives—judging vs. perceiving, extraversion vs. introversion, thinking vs. feeling, and intuition vs. sensing. The results tell how the people around you perceive you, how you see the world, your weaknesses and strengths, and your communication style.

MBTI is widely used in business settings, mainly aimed at improving self-understanding and understanding of co-workers. Below are the descriptions of the four polar preferences tested in MBTI:

- Extraversion Attitude (E), people will seek engagement with the outside world and others surrounding them. Introversion Attitude (I), people will seek encouragement from themselves.

- Sensing Perception (S) shows that the individual's perception is real, practical, immediate, and observable by the senses. Intuitive Perception (N) shows an individual's perception regarding implicit meanings, future observations, and symbolic or theoretical knowledge.

- Thinking Judgment (T) makes decisions based on rational reasoning and logical views. Feeling Judgement (F) makes decisions based on sentimentality, significance, or competing solutions.

- Judging (J) makes quick decisions, excels at planning and organizing, and will always prefer structural activities. Perceiving (P) curious, open to changes and foreignness, and adapt well to spontaneous situations.

These four categories are then combined to describe your overall personality. In the test, you will be given certain statements, and you and rate how much you agree, disagree, or have no opinion about them. The statements are often detailed by putting you in hypothetical situations, for example, "At social events, you rarely introduce yourself to new people." The test will then determine which traits are significant based on your choices.

Descriptions of each of the possible combinations of personality traits for the MBTI can be found at the following website:

https://www.verywellmind.com/the-myers-briggs-type-indicator-2795583

16 Personalities

The 16 Personalities is primarily used to assess an individual's sensitivity, emotional stability, self-reliance, openness to change, and perfectionism. Companies have used it to determine employee career development and progression. 16 Personalities is an evolved framework of MBTI. Now that you understand what MBTI is, the critical difference in 16 Personalities is the added dimension of identity—(A) for Assertive and (T) for Turbulent. The difference between these two identities is how we deal with problems in life and how we deal with progress, successes, and failures.

Assertive individuals are the "calm in the storm," self-assured, confident with progress, and resistant to stress. An assertive person may be perceived as apathetic or uncaring, but in reality, assertive people don't let nervousness or worry take over. This allows the assertive person to be more focused on goals than on challenges or problems that arise in a situation. Turbulent individuals, on the other hand, are perfectionists and aren't easily satisfied. Turbulent types will always strive for improvement, perfection, and success. When they don't achieve these, they will feel troubled. However, this shouldn't be seen as a negative trait. Turbulent people are highly motivated. By being a perfectionist, they can show the world just how impactful a strong-willed person can be.

Your Assertive or Turbulent identity dimension will be added to your corresponding personality type. For example, if you have an INTJ personality type and are assertive, that is, as an INTJ-A. You are an analytical thinker who is also confident in your work progress and doesn't mind paying extra attention to perfection. This additional identity dimension helps determine how you can thrive in your career. Assertive people may prefer to work in a calmer, more relaxed work environment but can thrive in busy, stressful workplaces. The 16 personalities test can be completed for free at the following website:

https://www.16personalities.com/free-personality-test

You will also be given your Myers-Briggs classification at the end of the free quiz.

The Big Five Personalities

Several independent researchers developed the Big Five Personalities test. At first, Gordon Allport created a list of about 4,500 terms explaining personality types, but many researchers thought that the list was too extensive; as a result, the Big Five Personalities emerged to describe the five core traits of personality types. Personality psychologists frequently recommend the Big Five Personalities test, also called the OCEAN personality test. The results are given as a percentage rather than a categorization describing each specific characteristic. The only disadvantage of this test is that it may be difficult for some to draw a definitive conclusion from their results.

The test also involves answering questions, but unlike the previous personality tests, this is a 300-question online test, so significant time is required to complete it and get a result. You would be asked to rate questions on a scale of "strongly agree" to "strongly disagree." The questions would say, "I am open to new experiences" or "I see myself as energetic." Depending on how much you disagree or agree with each statement, the test will determine which traits are more significant in you and rate you in five categories: openness, conscientiousness, extroversion, agreeableness, and neuroticism. You usually have one or two traits that dominate from these personality types. Let's take a look at the definitions for each category.

- Openness: People who score high in openness show high curiosity. People with high openness like challenges and exciting situations. They value new knowledge and always try to find new ways to discover things. Those scoring high in this trait are most likely disciplined. They exceed others' expectations and initiate actions as ordered. They love working in an organized environment and prefer planned over spontaneous activities.

- Conscientiousness: People who score high in conscientiousness are also defined by high levels of thoughtfulness. They have good impulse control and goal-directed behaviors. Conscientious people tend to be organized and pay great attention to details. They plan ahead, empathize with others' feelings, and are mindful of deadlines. These people spend time preparing to finish essential tasks right away and enjoy having a set schedule.

- Extroversion: This trait defines how an individual socializes with others. People who score high in the extroversion trait thrive in social situations. They appreciate teamwork and enjoy working with others toward the same goals.

- Agreeableness: Those who score high in agreeableness are the advocates. People with high agreeableness provide advice and insights to others. They are sympathetic, considerate, and sensitive to feelings. They will excel in group participation as they compromise easily.

- Neuroticism: This measure allows someone to see their emotional stability. High scores in neuroticism show higher anxiety and pessimism, while low scores show more calmness and stability. Some companies typically focus on low scores to help determine how much resilience a person could bring during stressful circumstances.

The big five personalities test can be completed at the following website:

https://brainmanager.io/tests/personality

Type A, B, C, and D Personalities

Two cardiologists, Ray Rosenman, and Meyer Friedman, developed this personality test in 1976 (Mcleod, 2023). Each category represents something different; the four personality types provide basic categorizations of certain traits. For example, those with Type A personalities, also known as Achievers, perform better under pressure, are goal-oriented, and are not afraid to take risks. Type B personalities, the Socializers, are outgoing and enthusiastic around other people. Individuals with Type C personalities are considered Thinkers, rely heavily on logical thinking, and are very detailed. Lastly, type D personalities, or The Supporter, are stable and cautious.

When completing this personality test, expect similar processes to the others, but in addition, you will be asked to fill out a personal profile form explaining how you work. The results will show a bar chart with a percentage for each type. The higher percentage shows the most dominant personality type. You can also score two or more combined traits from the four categories, called Type X personality. Let's take a look at each of the personality types:

- A type A person usually likes to be in control of their environment. They come up with practical solutions for problems and are focused on their goals. Type A personality traits can vary, but typically, they are passionate and ambitious with everything they do, making them highly competitive in their career. Since type A personalities are goal-oriented, they tend to be impatient and like everything fast-paced. This means they are better when working alone with more freedom.

- Type B people are those who are better at developing relationships. A type B person needs approval and acknowledgment from others. They are friendly, charismatic, and persuasive. Because they value relationships, socializing is an easy task for them. Usually, because of these traits, other people might think of them as self-centered, but this can be a good quality. Type B people are enthusiastic, friendly, and outgoing, and these traits will help in specific job fields, especially if the job requires them to be outgoing and energetic.

- Type C people are independent and organized individuals. They are highly logical, rational, factual, and accurate. Type C personalities still come with variable traits but are analytical, lawful, and detail-oriented. Type C people generally think a lot about progress and constantly ask questions, which makes it better for them to work in slow-paced environments that would need them to focus on details.

- Type D is a personality type associated with being caring, calm, patient, and easy-going. Type D people are observant and sensitive toward other people's feelings. However, they also have consistency, dependableness, and supportiveness; expressing their feelings to others can be challenging. That makes them less of an assertive person, often going along with what others are doing.

You can determine which of the four personality types you possess using the following website:

https://owlcation.com/social-sciences/what-is-your-personality-type-type-a-or-type-b

With the descriptions of these personality tests, I hope you've gained some new insights. Each personality type has some strengths and weaknesses. You can use this new knowledge to get a better glimpse of yourself, understand your qualities, and how those qualities can contribute to your future career choices. In the next chapter, we will discuss many specific careers and how they align with each of the personality types.

Chapter 2:

Choose the Career Path That's Right for You

For some, a career defines who and what they are. Some people may have found the perfect job for their lives, while others are still searching for one "match made in heaven." The fear of making the wrong decision can be paralyzing due to the fear of regretting your choice in the future. Similar to the pressure you may feel when choosing the "right" car. It can be overwhelming, and when staring down a path toward a specific job, you may fear that you will later feel like you've chosen the "wrong" path or have the urge to change directions down the line. Doing so can be very time-consuming and expensive in some cases. We are advised to follow our passions and pursue a college education that aligns with our interests, but what if you don't know what those interests are? With so many job opportunities, how can you navigate the confusing terrain of career planning? The fear of making the "wrong" decisions can be crippling, making you extremely cautious, fearing regret of your choice. However, determining which jobs you think are a match for yourself personally can alleviate much of the worry when choosing careers. In some cases, finding the "one perfect job" might need a bit of a detour or trial-and-error. Still, you should at least be "in the ballpark" regarding the type of career you want to end up with after considering your interests and personality type.

How you react to certain situations, work together with others, and your perceptions must be considered in your career. Personality types are powerful tools for getting to know oneself profoundly and why some people are better at being leaders while others excel more when working alone. Some people perform well in formal business, while others are more useful in creative fields. In this chapter, I will match each personality type to multiple suitable career fields.

Comparing Jobs with Personalities

Have you ever wondered why some people are so great at being artists? They produce creative works through painting, music, or sculpting consistently and with expertise. Some people belong in laboratories performing experiments and creating scientific breakthroughs. It connects with their inner qualities and how they channel this uniqueness in their work. You, too, can identify your unique qualities and let yourself shine in your work. Your expertise can be based on more than just skills alone but also on your style of socializing and how you perceive certain information.

Remember that your personality only acts as a guide to give you ideas about which path you may want to take, and, the truth is, only you can know what matches your interests, and you shouldn't only rely on generalizations of personality types. Personality types are large groups. However, people with the same personality types may still have differences due to their cultural backgrounds and personal beliefs and interests in general. These differences could matter more in terms of choosing a future career. In short, assigning specific careers for specific personality types might be too restrictive for certain people. For example, research may show that one personality type should have a high interest in sports, maybe 90%. That still leaves 10% of the people with that personality type that do not have a high interest in sports. Therefore, it is terrible advice to suggest that this personality type is always fit for sports. This is another reason why completing multiple personality tests is a good idea.

In this chapter, I will provide suggested careers for each personality type obtained in the four personality methods from chapter one. You will notice that the same career may be included with more than one personality type proving that specific jobs are not exclusive to just one personality category. Additionally, it is important to remember that interests, culture, and personal beliefs should also be considered when choosing a career.

The Best Career Choices for Myers-Briggs Type Indicator (MBTI) and 16 Personalities Types

INTJ (The Mastermind)-Introverted, Intuitive, Thinking, Judging

INTJ people are creative and strive for perfection. They will delve deeper into details and rely on intuition to solve problems. As introverted types, they usually prefer to work alone. They work better in non-social environments or those needing theoretical thinking.

INTJs are often described as visionary leaders who are very precise and focused on completing their goals. They excel in positions of authority where they can apply strategic thinking to overcome complicated challenges. They also tend to have a natural ability to understand the broader picture compared to others. They can, however, be seen as aloof or distant from others due to their tendency to focus on their thoughts and ideas. INTJs are critical of and have high expectations of others and themselves. Jobs that would fit with INTJ include:

- Project Manager

- Software Engineer/Developer

- Financial Advisor/Analyst

- Marketing Strategist

- Professor

INTP (The Logician)-Introverted, Intuitive, Thinking, Perceiving

INTPs are deep thinkers; they like to experiment with ideas and rely on logic. More often than not, they will always try to uncover the truth and will question everything until they find the most plausible answer. With qualities like these, it would be best for INTPs to pursue careers that would let them innovate and solve complex problems. INTPs are also well-known for their adaptability and flexibility. They are open-minded and willing to accept opposing viewpoints, even if they eventually disagree. They frequently address challenges rationally and objectively, using analytical thinking to find solutions. INTPs can struggle when making decisions because they often overanalyze choices and may need to work on making them. They can be seen as reserved or quiet due to their tendency to be lost in their thoughts. They can, however, be friendly and engaged with those who share the same interests and passions. Some jobs that would fit with INTP include:

- Research/Academia
- Scientist
- Philosopher
- Architect
- Professor
- Translator/Interpreter

INFP (The Mediator)-Introverted, Intuitive, Feeling, Perceiving

Intelligent, imaginative, and open-minded, INFPs are deeply in tune with their feelings and personality. They are compassionate and enjoy doing everything that challenges creative thinking. However, they most likely dislike an organized routine or something that hinders their imaginative qualities. INFPs are usually regarded as contemplative and reflective dreamers. They have a vast inner world and are frequently drawn to artistic pursuits, such as music, writing, or drawing. They may need help with practical activities or long-term planning since they can be overwhelmed with details. They can also be very sensitive and take criticism or rejection personally. However, they can be good friends and partners who are committed to the ones they care about. INFP types would be best to choose careers that rely on passion and personal expression, such as:

- Visual Artist
- Musician
- Creative Writing
- Activist
- Educational Consultant

INFJ (The Sage)-Introverted, Intuitive, Feeling, Judging

Although introverted, INFJs tend to excel in teamwork. They like helping others and rely on personal principles, integrity, and ideological thinking. INFJs are known to be thoughtful and will be cautious with each step they take. INFJs are known for having strong personal ideals as well as understanding others. They have a strong sense of purpose and are driven to change the world positively as silent leaders through their words and actions. They are charismatic and extremely empathetic to other people's wants and feelings. Jobs that best fit an INFJ include:

- Medical Laboratory Professional
- Personal Counselor
- Social Worker
- Environmental Scientist

- Psychiatrist

ISTP (The Tinkerer)-Introverted, Sensing, Thinking, Perceiving

ISTPs are determined and energetic and will let nothing stop them from achieving their goals. ISTPs are known as those who are adamant and openly honest. ISTPs have an individualistic mindset and would always prefer action. "Talk less, do more" would be their motto. ISTPs are generally described as quiet, reserved people who prefer to work alone. They have a good eye for detail and are incredibly observant, sometimes able to spot details others overlook. They are highly adaptive and thrive when thinking and action are required. ISTPs are also drawn to high-risk pursuits, making them a good fit for sports or other adrenaline-fueled activities. ISTPs can thrive in the careers listed below:

- Athlete

- Detective

- Forensic Scientist

- Pilot

- Firefighter

ISTJ (The Archivist)-Introverted, Sensing, Thinking, Judging

ISTJs are great at being reliable, meticulous, and sharp in their work commitment, and show consistency and authority. They are hard workers, independent, and make decisions based on careful consideration. ISTJs are usually described as dependable people who value structure and stability. They have a strong work ethic and are well-regarded for being consistent. Sometimes, ISTJs can struggle with change or new situations, and they are not the most outspoken individuals, but they show love and care through actions and practical gestures. ISTJs should try careers that support their sense of commitment, such as:

- Military

- Police

- Accountant

- Legal Counsel

- Medical Field (any job)

ISFP (The Adventurer)-Introverted, Sensing, Feeling, Perceiving

Aesthetics fuel their lives. ISFPs pay attention to aesthetic pleasure and would try to present themselves accordingly. They have a passion for beauty, though they don't care much for wealth or power. ISFPs are defined as independent, self-sufficient people who appreciate freedom and autonomy. They are spontaneous and live-in-the-moment kinds of people. ISFPs are sensitive when it comes to caring for others. Being attentive to others, ISFPs would prefer fields that would help them to express themselves artistically as well as show off aesthetic qualities; ISFPs fit well in careers such as:

- Fashion Designer
- Professional Photographer
- Music
- Fine Arts
- Massage Therapist

ISFJ (The Defender)-Introverted, Sensing, Feeling, Judging

ISFJs have a great desire to help other people. They are highly responsible, committed, supportive, hardworking, and efficient. They want to avoid being acknowledged and would prefer to work behind the scenes rather than gain a position of authority. ISFJs are described as warm and loving people who value harmony and stability. Because they emphasize the "correct" way, ISFJs often struggle with being overly critical or perfectionistic. They may also avoid confrontation and disagreement, preferring to keep their relationship harmonious, but they are loyal and supportive of others. A few careers for ISFJs include:

- Social Worker
- Customer Service
- Human Resources
- Police Officer
- Teacher

ENTJ (The General)-Extroverted, Intuitive, Thinking, Judging

ENTJs are the leader type. They like authority and practice getting things done. They are natural leaders, strategic, and highly logical. They have high motivation to solve problems and have reasonable confidence. ENTJs have a natural ability to take charge and lead others because they are analytical and logical thinkers who can easily spot patterns and connections that others may miss. Because they expect high performance and excellent standards, ENTJs may need help with being accepting of the needs of others. They may also be impatient or dismissive of people who don't share their visions. However, they are still visionary and innovative leaders who can inspire others. ENTJs are perfect in jobs that require team-leading and careful planning, such as:

- Executive
- Lawyer
- Entrepreneurship
- Politician
- Business Strategist

ENTP (The Debater)-Extroverted, Intuitive, Thinking, Perceiving

ENTPs approach everything with great confidence. They are bold, sarcastic, and witty, with just the right amount of creativity. They love challenges and taking risks. ENTPs may struggle with being argumentative or rebellious, as they enjoy playing devil's advocate and may occasionally upset others with their debate-like approach. They may also be quickly bored or distracted; they are highly creative and innovative people who can come up with solutions in challenging situations. ENTPs are quick-thinkers, which makes them suitable to work in fields such as:

- Politics

- Public Relations

- Systems Analyst

- Sales Agent

- Film Producer

- Computer Programmer

ENFP (The Optimist)-Extroverted, Intuitive, Feeling, Perceiving

It can be hard to determine the perfect career match for an ENFP as they can be the definition of a "free spirit." However, the good thing is that ENFPs are not afraid to try new things, even things that seem entirely foreign. They will find everything interesting and are enthusiastic about diving deeper into new experiences. ENFPs are often described as eager and optimistic people seeking new experiences and opportunities. They are very creative and imaginative, often seeing things from multiple perspectives. ENFPs can struggle with being overly idealistic or impulsive because they are frequently divided between various options. They may also be quickly overwhelmed because they have a lot of energy and want to take on too many things simultaneously; they are adaptive and resilient people who can recover from setbacks and hardships. They are independent and energetic, which is why some of the careers fit for ENFPs include:

- Film Director

- Broadcaster/Newscaster

- Screenwriting

- Journalist

- Real Estate Agent

ENFJ (The Guide) - Extroverted, Intuitive, Feeling, Judging

As people who stand true to self-perseverance, ENFJs are valuable due to their quality, reliability, and being a people-helper. They are open to strong ideas and values. They love being the center of attention; they are diplomatic, logical, and cooperative. ENFJs are warm and social people. They have a natural ability to connect with others and form relationships quickly. ENFJs may struggle with being overly sensitive or emotional at times. They also habitually focus on other people's emotions and become overwhelmed by their feelings. They may also be self-sacrificing as they prioritize others' needs over their own. They are, however, very organized and determined people who can take charge and make tough decisions when necessary. That's why some of the jobs good for ENFJs include:

- Motivational Speaker

- Politician
- Human Resources
- Advertising
- Diplomat

ESTJ (The Administrator)-Extroverted, Sensing, Thinking, Judging

ESTJs honor responsibilities and traditions. They love working in fields that give them structure and consistency. ESTJs value loyalty and honesty and have a realistic mindset. They would be in charge because they are good at guiding others to achieve common goals. They make quick and logical decisions and often tackle issues head-on without hesitation.

ESTJs are dependable people who are well-organized and efficient in their work. They are naturally gifted in handling a variety of challenging situations. Because they have a strong sense of morality, they may have difficulties considering outside perspectives. ESTJs may be viewed as uptight or inflexible. They may also be too controlling since they always prefer to have things done their way. Nonetheless, they are trustworthy and committed people who take their duties seriously. Career fields that are suitable matches for ESTJs are:

- Judge
- Pharmacist
- Insurance
- Lawyer
- Project Manager
- Detective

ESTP (The Daredevil)-Extroverted, Sensing, Thinking, Perceiving

For some, ESTPs might appear short-sighted in decision-making; however, that is one of their unique qualities to embrace. ESTPs tend to be oriented toward valuing even minor achievements. As a result, they thrive in fast-paced work since they are consistent in their objectives and always want to be quick in making decisions. ESTPs are action-oriented and focused on the current moment. They may sometimes struggle with being impulsive and reckless since they habitually act rapidly without fully considering the consequences. They may also need to focus more on immediate results, so they need help planning for the long term. However, they are highly adaptive and resilient individuals who can manage problems easily manage issues to be resourceful, so careers that would be a good match for ESTPs include:

- Acting

- Reporter

- Banker

- Management

- Paramedic

ESFJ (The Caregiver)-Extroverted, Sensing, Feeling, Judging

Altruistic and well-organized, ESFJs don't shy away from routines and love to serve others when it comes to their responsibilities. They will be quick to take action, but they also show attentiveness and enthusiasm. ENFJs are called Caregivers because they are mindful of others' feelings. They gravitate toward traditions and love to be in a role where they need to be social. ESFJs are compassionate and caring people with a natural ability to demonstrate appreciation. They may struggle with being overly concerned with others' needs at their own cost. However, they are efficient individuals who can easily manage tasks and obligations. They generally find fulfillment in others around them. Some of the careers that would be perfect for ESFJs are:

- Nursing
- Healthcare worker
- Receptionist
- Catering
- Counselor

ESFP (The Entertainer)-Extroverted, Sensing, Feeling, Perceiving

ESFPs are expressive, playful, and full of life. ESFPs love the excitement and meaningful interactions with others. They love making every situation lively and always look for a chance to shine. ESFPs are known for their energy, spontaneity, and ability to connect with others. They are fun-loving people who are keenly aware of their surroundings. They like to live in the present moment and appreciate life valuing instant pleasures over long-term goals; ESFPs often struggle with being too impulsive or sensation-seeking. They may also quickly get bored and struggle with repetitive activities. Nonetheless, they are highly adaptable, flexible, and easily adjust to new surroundings. ESFPs are fit for the following careers:

- Acting

- Tour Guide

- Theatre

- Stand-up Comedian

- Interior Designer

Choosing careers based on your personality's strengths can help you figure out which path you want to take but be sure to identify your interests as well. Are you a creative person that likes abstract ideas, or are you a person who is disciplined and prefers to work in an organized environment?

The Best Career Choices for Each Big Five Personality Traits

Companies might use the Big Five personality test when hiring new employees. This test helps determine who might fit with their employees based on how they function in specific workplace situations. Aside from your salary and responsibilities, identifying whether professions are suited for you may require some information from your Big Five Personalities score. If you are conscientious, you should work in a formal sector rather than in casual settings and be surrounded by large groups of people.

Career Choices for High Openness

Those who score high in openness will thrive in a highly open career, working in fields that give them more freedom to create and invent. Some of the careers that would match high openness are:

- Fashion design
- Interior design
- Writing
- Tour guide
- Entrepreneurship
- Lawyer
- Pilot

These careers will allow them to explore the world while at the same time appreciating their open-mindedness and imagination.

Career Choices for High Conscientiousness

Conscientious people are well-organized and careful. They like everything in tip-top shape and like following planned schedules. Some of the careers that would be a match for high conscientiousness are:

- Freelance writing
- Photography

- Visual design
- Doctor
- Psychologist
- Teacher
- Project manager
- Laboratory scientist

These jobs usually require careful planning and tight deadlines.

Career Choices for High Extroversion

Extroverted people are enthusiastic and energetic around other people. They will fit in with careers that need them to be assertive and friendly. Since they are easy-going and social, jobs that fit this personality type are:

- Public relations
- Sales
- Hosting
- Advertising
- News casting

These jobs require their charismatic traits to help gain others' attention.

Career Choices for High Agreeableness

Having a high score in agreeableness doesn't mean these individuals agree with what everyone says. The agreeable trait means these people are sympathetic and caring toward other people. They have a natural talent for being a good mediator. Since their characteristics involve exercising empathy and sympathy for other people, careers that will fit this personality type are:

- Nursing or other healthcare jobs
- Counselor
- Teacher
- Non-profit organization

These types of careers involve sensible teamwork.

Career Choices for High Neuroticism

Scoring high in neuroticism isn't necessarily negative. Highly neurotic people tend to show higher anxiety and emotional instability rates than their low neurotic counterparts. This means highly neurotic people are perfect in jobs with calmer surroundings, such as:

- Yoga instructor
- Massage therapist
- Librarian

- Freelance work

On the other hand, people who scored low in neuroticism can fit into jobs such as:

- Nursing or other healthcare jobs
- Social worker
- Customer service

Low neurotic people are perfect for jobs that are a bit pressing or stressful, as they have better emotional control. Sometimes, people have mixed traits that make their personality type unique. For example, you can be both conscientious and highly open. You can be self-disciplined but also creative and imaginative. Always consider each aspect of your personality when choosing a potential career.

The Best Career Choices for A, B, C, and D Personality Types

Career Choices for Type A Personality

Type A individuals are generally workaholics. The nature of a Type A person is fast-paced and stressful at times. Jobs that will fit this personality type are:

- Software Engineer
- Statistician
- Executive Assistant

- Medical Laboratory Professional

These jobs require them to be detailed, precise, and organized. These positions also allow them to work most of the time independently, giving them more freedom in managing their workload without putting the responsibility on another person or a big team.

Career Choices for Type B Personality

Type B individuals take pride in contributing to other people. Careers requiring them to be collaborative are most beneficial, including:

- Teacher

- Consultant

- Coaching service

These fields will allow Type B people to collaborate with clients, help them overcome specific problems, and help them take action in their lives.

Career Choices for Type C Personality

Type C individuals tend to be objective, skeptical, and rely heavily on logical thinking. They are calm and reserved and prefer solitary environments. Careers that fit into this personality type are:

- Systems Administrator

- Engineer

- Data Scientist

- Financial Analyst

These jobs require them to be analytical, meticulous, and careful.

Career Choices for Type D Personality

Since Type D individuals are generally supportive toward other people, careers that would match this personality type are:

- Psychologist

- Healthcare worker

- Public relations

These careers require someone to be up close and personal with others. While several examples of suitable career choices have been given, remember that the personality types above are generalized. They are only intended to help you understand particular personality types and how they can operate effectively in various jobs. You may have a combination of multiple personality attributes, all of which need to be considered.

Chapter 3:

Get Perspective Through Research and Advice

In your life, I'm sure you have come across other people with a career that matches your interests. Someone might have inspired you to take the same path when you were younger. It could be anyone, family members, teachers, acquaintances, or others. You can benefit from these connections with other people by learning more about a specific job from another person's perspective. You can ask them what they do in their profession, what a typical day or week would be like in that career, what vital characteristics or talents they have needed to be successful, what significant challenges they or others they know may have faced, what kind of salary is usually offered for positions in the field, or how much formal education is needed. The internet should also be a source of research due to the availability of blogs and websites.

Getting information about experiences from other people is valuable in helping you prepare for the "real-world experience." If your dream job requires you to master a specific skill, you could start planning your path by training in this skill early on. It would also be advisable to attend job fairs which may be held online or in person. Attending events like these will provide you with more knowledge about the careers or careers that interest you. Occasionally, job fair events also give direct interviews or presentations by people in specific professional careers, providing information on the steps necessary in preparing for future employment and how those careers fit a person's everyday life and long-term goals. In this chapter, I will explore some crucial questions you must ask yourself before deciding on a career.

Things to Consider Before Choosing a Career

Talents, Skills, and Personality

We discussed in the previous chapters that identifying your personality should be the first indicator of your chosen career path. We have also discussed some of the talents associated with each of the personality types and which career choices are the most agreeable for each.

The talents, skills, and interests someone possesses will also play a significant role in their success in any career. Although talents and skills are often used interchangeably, they aren't the same. Fundamentally, talents are your natural born qualities. In other words, a part of your personality (e.g., introverted, hardworking, outgoing), while skills are something you can learn and practice (e.g., good communication, engineering, cleaning a cut properly).

Consider pilots; this career requires discipline, attention to detail, and fast thinking. However, you wouldn't expect these people to have been born with the ability to fly. They had to go through intense training to learn and master their skills. Airline companies choose employees based on a combination of their inherent traits, ensuring they can handle stressful situations while in the air, as well as the level of skill they possess in flying planes.

It is best to align your inherent talents with your learned skills when entering the workforce in any career. Identifying your talents and skills early will give you a jump-start in choosing a suitable future profession. Take pride in your abilities and interests because your skills and passions go a long way in having a successful career. Do you like drawing? Are you particularly interested in science? You can start with these initial interests and then move on to learning how to hone the appropriate skills as you get ready to choose a career.

Finding out what you are good at can be challenging, however. If you are having trouble, you don't have to worry. With enough effort, you can learn and become proficient at any skill you are interested in. In addition to skills, knowledge is usually also required for employment in any job, so a desire for learning is essential to succeed in a career. BUSINESS INSIDER reports that the average person works 90,000 hours in their lifetime; consider how you want to spend that time (Premack, 2018). Where you choose to work is where you decide to grow, not just where you choose to get paid. Align your career to your talents, personality, and skills to help you decide where to go next.

Education and Training

Most employers value people with a lot of experience and knowledge. In some companies, you will be required to hold a college degree, but before deciding on the type of institution to attend for a degree, consider questions such as:

- What is the most effective way for you to learn?

- How long can you commit to attending classes?

- What kind of education or knowledge do you need for your chosen career?

Believe it or not, pursuing a successful career can sometimes require more than four years of formal education at a university. Even if the career you plan to pursue requires a four-year degree, there are other options besides entering university. Additionally, many attractive, high-paying careers do not require years of education. Some need only one year or two years of formal education, and many successful professionals attended community college or trade school to learn the skills and obtain diplomas, licenses, and certificates qualifying them to compete for high-paying jobs. Such careers include medical laboratory technology, welding, HVAC (heating, ventilating, and air conditioning), automotive repair, mechatronics, horticulture, and landscaping.

Different people have different learning styles. Some prefer to learn hands-on, while others prefer learning theories first and then applying them later. Whichever way you learn best, proper training will give you adequate knowledge and skills for your chosen career. Suppose you are not able to pursue formal education right away. In that case, you can try volunteering or internships to get more information or experience in the workforce. At the same time, you can still be enrolled in high school, giving you a "jump start" on career experience in a particular industry before committing to formal education. In addition, you'd have direct experience with a job and a chance to "test the waters," so to speak, to determine if you'd love a particular line of work. More importantly, internships and volunteer positions are great to put on your resume.

Another solution to getting started on your path to the job of your dreams before attending formal on-campus college classes is to attend classes online. Online courses are great, especially if you prefer more flexible learning hours. Nowadays, some students prefer online classes due to their decreased costs or more course variety. This will also be a great choice if you are currently working one job and are interested in learning something new in preparation for a career change. Online classes are also individualized, meaning the system works at your pace. They can even allow you to collaborate with students from other locations without physically meeting. While known for their flexibility, online classes also teach you time management skills, having complete control over your schedule, when to attend, how much time it takes to complete an assignment, and more.

There are so many educational options out there for you to choose from. You should determine what type of education or training you would need through research before you pursue your chosen career. You will learn more about education options in the next chapter, but first, you must consider what type of education or training you need and what type of education you can commit to.

Your Goals and Purpose

Like other things we do in life, everything has a purpose. What purpose do you have in mind before your career? Why do you think this career path would fit you? Understanding why you want to pursue a specific path while picking a career is critical.

90,000 hours is a lot of time, so make sure what you're pursuing aligns with your goals. Choosing a career with a specific end goal will make you feel more knowledgeable and prepared in the long run.

When assessing goals, they can be divided into two categories, personal and professional. Personal goals include motivations such as buying a house, owning a car, or buying a new phone. Professional goals are more inclined toward the professional expertise and milestones you want to achieve over time such as owning or starting a business, becoming a CEO, or writing a best-selling novel.

To start, you can ask yourself questions like:

- What are my personal goals?

- What are my professional goals?

- What careers will allow me to pursue my interests, use my talents and skills, and achieve both my personal and professional goals?

- Which career(s) also match my personal values?

These questions will help you align your goals with the career you want to pursue. After you've defined your long-term goals, you should begin by outlining some of your short-term goals. For example, say your long-term goal is to own a successful gourmet restaurant. To reach this objective, create a to-do list before opening the business. You can begin by learning to cook professionally and then gain certification in culinary studies. From there, all you have to do is work your way up and establish a reputation and gain financing to start your restaurant.

The power of goal-setting extends beyond simply having something to do. There is a science behind how we view goals and what happens when we achieve them, no matter how little. According to a study by James (2019), if you allow yourself to be content with the small things you have accomplished, you will be more goal-oriented in the future since you are molding your brain to achieve more goals. Your goal could be as modest as cleaning your room. Once reaching this goal, you will feel rewarded and motivated to achieve more goals. Setting these goals may be difficult for some, which is understandable. If you need help figuring out where to begin, start with small self-improvement like getting up at 7 a.m. daily, jogging daily, etc. After that, you can focus on the bigger goals you wish to achieve. It doesn't matter if this takes you a few months or years; starting small and building a habit usually works better than setting lofty goals that are very difficult to reach initially and getting discouraged.

If you are already working and determine that your current job will not help you reach your goals, it may be time to change careers and explore other options. Switching career paths might be needed in certain circumstances. It may seem scary, but believe me, it's doable. I will cover more about changing careers in the following chapters, but before we do that, you should determine your goals as early as possible, preferably before you choose a career to pursue.

Employment Opportunities

The job market is constantly changing. This factor will affect employment opportunities and should be a serious consideration in choosing a career. As the world evolves, so do its economic systems, which creates a new variety of options. Companies are constantly adapting to new technologies and consumer demands. As a result, they want to hire motivated and skilled individuals to join their team. As a job seeker, you must prepare for this. The creation of new careers and the elimination of obsolete ones as a result of technological advancements can influence the career path you choose. You must choose education and training that will allow you to adapt to the shifting job market, providing you with unique skills that will make you stand out from the crowd, no matter your chosen job. It can be discouraging to find out that a career you desire has had a decrease in demand in recent years. Career longevity lies in the ability of a job to change along with technological advances. Furthermore, the COVID-19 outbreak has caused a global economic recession. Some countries may have experienced a temporary slump as the pandemic continued into 2021 and impacted major economic sectors.

According to statistics, the U.S. economy will add 8.3 million jobs between 2021 and 2031. Overall employment is expected to rise roughly 0.5% yearly, much more than the 0.1% annual growth reported in the previous decade, 2011-2021. (Bureau of Labor Statistics, 2022). These numbers reveal that while jobs and employment have continued to rise quickly, the pandemic has acted as a catalyst that is still likely to disrupt long-term employment demand in some industries. Nevertheless, there is no shortage of options for committed job seekers, whether in traditional professions like healthcare and education or growing sectors like renewable energy and artificial intelligence. It would be best to be inventive and persistent in adapting to the world by thoroughly researching the opportunities that will provide you with the skills you need to make yourself stand out from others and determine whether a specific career will still be relevant in future years.

Work-Life Balance

What is work-life balance? We often consider it a trade-off between how much time a person spends at work and how much time they spend on themselves. Aside from work, we have many other things to do: cooking, house chores, working out, or simply hanging out with friends and family. We all know that working too much wouldn't be good physically and mentally, yet sometimes it's hard to figure out how much is too much.

The boundary between "work" and "life" is becoming increasingly blurred in today's world due to the expansion of remote work. It doesn't help that humanity has experienced one of the most devastating worldwide pandemics in recent years. These events resulted in poor time management skills and distorted the "work-life balance" concept. When the COVID-19 pandemic hit, our home life also became our work life. Many of us began to work, eat, and rest in one location using the electronics in our homes. This has become highly convenient for some people. Rush hour is a thing of the past for many. You can still play video games 10 minutes before starting work or class if you are a student, and be ready to attend at the click of a button when the teacher shows up.

This sense of "extra time" can lead people to devote more time to work. You don't need to wake up extra early tomorrow to go to class, so you put in an all-nighter to finish today's assignment, staying up so late that by the time you go to bed, there are only three hours left before sunrise. Slowly, this can become a habit, disrupting your work-life balance, a prominent aspect of the "new normal" era. Because of many misconceptions, some people still need help to maintain an acceptable work-life balance. Keys to a healthy balance include limiting overtime, knowing your ideal work hours, and knowing how to use the spare time that exists when there is no commute to work.

We often believe that by working more hours, we will be more productive; however, it's quite the opposite. Stanford University examined a person's productivity after specific periods spent working. [work] output decreases as hours increase" (Pencavel, 2015). Once we reach a certain point of working hours, our productivity will drop. This explains why some people who work harder, or "workaholics," suffer more from exhaustion, burnout, and stress. Before you start diving into your career, it's essential to learn about time management. You will have a healthy work-life balance with good time management skills. However, there is no ideal way to maintain this balance since everyone's life differs. You may need to play around with your schedule before determining your best routine.

Just like setting career goals, it's better to start small with your goals for work-life balance. If your main objective in improving work-life balance is to reduce screen time by 50%, it frustrates you because you may need your gadgets a lot more than that to finish your work. Habits won't change overnight, and you need to be patient. You're more likely to stick to a new routine if you start with small steps. For example, reduce screen time for at least three minutes daily, then increase those numbers as you get used to it. During that three-minute break, you can do something else to keep you away from smartphones or other electronics, like reading a book, a light workout, or simply detaching yourself from the virtual world. Below are other things you can do to maintain an excellent work-life balance, such as:

1. **Set a schedule for different tasks**. Determine when to check or respond to messages, emails, and notifications. Set time for intensive work hours, and set time for when you need to take a break and remember your eating schedule. You can do this by setting timers

so that your activities will be better organized. Moreover, you'll have better control of your work and rest hours so you can learn to believe.

2. **Combine work with leisure tasks.** If you have assignments, meetings, or work at home, combine tasks while doing other things. Read your textbooks outside, play with your pet while doing assignments, or walk while in a meeting. This might seem to distract some people, but the idea is to keep yourself from working too hard for extended periods and becoming burnt out.

3. **Figure out how you can work effectively.** Do you prefer to work consistent hours, or do you like to work in short bursts of energy? Everyone's productivity is different, and you should embrace how you work. The Pomodoro technique is a popular time management method that allows you to alternate between focused work sessions and frequent short breaks (Boogaard, 2023). It's a well-known "productivity hack," mainly for working or attending classes from home. To use this method, you typically need to devote 25 minutes to focus work, followed by a five-minute short break. Repeat this process until you finish an entire task or project.

4. **End work at a particular time.** Whether you choose remote work or office work, dividing your time between when you should be working and taking a break is essential. If you work from the office, finish your tasks as needed so you will go home unburdened. If you work from home, set the alarm to remind you that work for today is completed.

5. **Go to a meal with friends, family, or co-workers.** This can help deepen your relationships with others and help you to eat properly throughout the day. Sometimes when we're too busy, we must remember to eat, squeeze in some time with the people around us, and eat lunch together. It could be as short as grabbing a quick meal and returning to work.

6. **Use technology to your advantage.** Today, living without our smartphones and other gadgets is practically impossible. You can use these to your advantage. You can use mobile apps that block out distractions (like notifications, messages, etc.) while still being able to use your necessary work tools. If available, restrict your work to another device and eliminate distracting applications such as instant messengers, social media, and internet browsers.

7. **Take some time off.** Whether you're going on a vacation or want to spend all day alone at home, sometimes you need to recharge and return to work feeling refreshed. Set some time off to nurture yourself and avoid overworking.

8. **Find a hobby.** Hobbies are helpful to keep your mind off stressful things. When you have some spare time, do any activities that you enjoy. It could be sports, reading a book, gardening, or many other things. Try to do activities that wouldn't remind you of work or school.

9. **Communicate.** Sometimes, communication is needed for you to achieve a work-life balance. You should communicate and set some boundaries with co-workers or superiors about your ideal working hours, weekend

policies, or out-of-office messaging. If you don't want other people to message you about work outside working hours, you must discuss this with them.

10. **Consider if your work culture supports your boundaries**. Is your supervisor accommodating to your requests for time off? Are your co-workers understanding and respectful of your personal space? Some work cultures need to be more considerate of your individual needs. Some may still call you on weekends or after work hours. Analyze whether this culture would support your work-life balance; if not, you may need to seek other jobs that are more supportive of balancing work and life.

11. **Seek professional help from counselors or therapists**. Getting professional advice should be considered. If you're feeling overwhelmed by the quantity of work you've been doing and don't know how to handle everything to obtain work-life balance, talk it over with a counselor or therapist and seek their guidance. An expert can assist you in identifying your issues and making the necessary changes based on your needs.

While choosing a career may appear complicated, careful consideration and detailed planning are just what you need. In addition to evaluating your abilities, talents, and skills, you should consider long-term goals and opportunities when deciding on a career path. In addition, you should look for work cultures that promote work-life balance, as this is crucial for maintaining a healthy and productive lifestyle. Balancing personal needs with job expectations can be challenging, but prioritizing self-care, setting boundaries with others, and communicating can be significantly impactful. Finding a work-life balance technique that works for you may take time and effort, but the results are worth it. By establishing a healthy balance between work or school and personal life, you can be more productive and satisfied in classes if you attend from home or in your future profession.

Chapter 4:

Plan Your Pathway

So far, you have learned about different personality types, what careers may fit with each of them, and what other aspects you should consider before choosing a career. Now, it's time to move on to the start of your career planning. When we discuss planning, what usually comes to mind is education. The majority of people attended formal education through high school. From there, high school graduates can start looking for jobs or part-time activities to fill their time until they decide to move forward with higher education or other career options.

Companies frequently seek experienced, competent, and knowledgeable individuals, and formal education can provide you with the relevant qualifications or degrees to assist you in fulfilling the hiring requirements. Companies may look for employees with experience in a specific field, and completing educational coursework can provide you with some of this experience. Higher education is an excellent option for starting on the path to a long-term career now. After high school graduation, it's easy to feel overwhelmed and unsure where to begin at this stage because of the many potential pathways you can take, which is why it is a good idea to start the decision-making process well before graduation. Your class choices will influence your journey and how you shape your future. For some, career planning may not begin until after they have completed a college degree. Additional job options are available if you have recently graduated from high school or university and are still figuring things out. The choices may differ slightly, but there is still time for you to land a job.

In this chapter, we will begin with educational options such as community college, trade school, university, or military institutions. I will also provide a breakdown of each option, similarities, and differences between the systems, and highlight some high-paying careers that do not require a four-year college degree.

Pursuing Higher Education

Obtaining a college degree can bring you many benefits. First, education gives you the necessary knowledge and expertise to find positions in a highly competitive job market. Having exceptional skills and knowledge from advanced academic institutions also brings you more job opportunities, higher salaries, and better job security. Higher education can also help you develop critical thinking and broaden your perspectives, and communication skills, which are essential in most professional environments. After high school, you may decide to attend community college, a trade school, or university, join the military, or even opt to enter the workforce directly. Your choice will depend on your needs and vision for your future.

Starting College While in High School

You might be thinking; CAN I DO THAT? You certainly can. Education is now more accessible than ever. You can begin college while still in high school to earn credits before graduating. You can do this while taking required high school classes, on summer break, or by taking online courses. Gaining college credits before you even set foot on campus is highly beneficial; you may be able to complete college in less than four years, fit in a double major, or make time to study abroad. High school students can participate in a variety of programs, including:

- **Advanced Placement (A.P.) Testing**

    A.P. classes are collegiate-level classes taught in high school and vary in their offerings. Some schools begin offering A.P. testing in sophomore year, while others may introduce A.P. testing to first-year students. These classes work similarly to college, using a syllabus and college-level reading materials, giving students more competency and higher education. These classes also have midterm and final exams and are evaluated on a scale of one to five. Most schools require a score of at least three to award college credit. Students will obtain a high school credit regardless of their performance on the A.P. exam.

- **College-Level Examination Program (CLEP)**

    CLEP requires students to achieve an acceptable minimum score on the exam to earn credits. Unlike A.P. testing, there is no class. The test is timed, and specific CLEP study resources are available online. Students can prepare for the exam by taking free online prep courses. Each college has its own list of classes for which CLEP examinations count as credit hours, so students should consult with their intended college before starting this program.

- **Excelsior College Examinations (ECEs)**

    ECEs, like CLEPs, are competency exams that do not require classroom instruction. It is worth mentioning that only nursing exams have been recognized by the American Council on Education's College Credit Recommendation Services (ACE CREDIT). Before the test, students will be given materials and around six months to prepare. ECEs can also be used by working adults to further their careers, and students from other schools can take these tests to transfer credits to Excelsior University, a private online university based in Albany, New York.

- **The International Baccalaureate (I.B.) Diploma Programme**

    This is a curriculum in which students are guided in the completion of an extended essay similar to a short thesis paper. It is advised that students learn theory and foreign languages. Test scores are reviewed by external instructors at the end of the program and assigned numerical grades ranging from one to forty-five. A score of twenty-four or more is considered appropriate for a passing grade. Although no college credits are offered, this program prepares students for the challenging academic life of college. The I.B. Diploma Programme may help applicants with highly competitive university admissions processes stand out. You can use the following link to find out which high schools in your state offer the I.B. Diploma Programme: **https://blog.prepscholar.com/international-baccalaureate-schools-in-us-complete-list**

- **Online Courses**

    Online courses are incredibly accessible, especially now that today's technology encourages online and independent learning more than ever. Prices for online courses at a regular academic university are roughly the same as for classroom study. However, some campuses may charge extra per class, so browse around before selecting online courses.

- **Summer College Programs**

    Summer college programs provide students with an introduction to campus life. It may resemble a summer camp but also offers a taste of campus life and the college environment. Nearly all areas of study are made available, and you will also live in dorms and eat on campus. Although these programs are expensive, most schools offer some financial assistance, and some provide full scholarships. These programs can be helpful for someone undecided about attending university and living on campus.

- **Dual Enrollment Programs**

    Probably the most commonly used method of gaining college credit while still in high school is dual enrollment. Students can choose dual enrollment programs, in which they receive credit for each class at both their high school and an associated community college. Students can complete enough college credits through dual enrollment that when they graduate with a high school diploma, they also receive a two-year associate degree from the community college, free of charge. Another benefit of dual enrollment programs is that most community colleges work with in-state universities to ensure that the general education credits completed at the community college will be accepted as general education credits at the university level and can be counted toward a four-year degree, as well.

Attending Community College or Trade School

Let's first discuss community college. Usually referred to as the "junior" college, you can earn an associate degree which can be transferred to a bachelor's degree by transferring credits to a four-year university program, but many degrees also provide the skills and certifications required to enter the workforce after only two years of education. In community college, you will learn some practical skills needed for a future career, typically including theoretical studies.

Colleges are often divided into two primary divisions: university transfer and career and technical programs.

The university transfer division commonly includes departments that provide general education classes, including English, psychology, mathematics, history, and other transferable topics, to universities for a four-year degree. The career and technical division includes departments providing education and skills training to graduate workforce-ready professionals in medical laboratory technology, welding, landscaping, nursing, computer technology, animal care, automotive, culinary arts, and many more.

Most degrees from community colleges are designed to be completed in two years but vary depending on each student's course load from semester to semester. In addition, you can build your schedule to fit a work schedule if needed, with options for morning classes, evening classes, and full-time or part-time. Community colleges are typically state-subsidized, which means they have minimal tuition and are likely the most cost-effective educational option available. While reports say typical fees are about $1,865 per semester compared to an average of $12,853 at university as an in-state student (Hanson, 2022), tuition fees are still determined by the program, the state, and the college you're attending.

A trade school, also known as a technical or vocational school, offers programs that provide you with hands-on experience in a particular career. The education at a trade school will focus on specific skills and knowledge without the general education classes required at community college. Many trade school programs require you to complete an apprenticeship, in which you work in your chosen career, to learn more about the occupation by working in the field with other professionals. The skills taught in trade schools usually relate to design, utilizing, and understanding tools. Jobs in skilled crafts usually include blacksmithing, carpentry, electrical work, and mechanical engineering, among others. Most programs in trade schools will take less than a year to finish, but some programs with higher-level technical skill requirements will require a year or two to complete.

There are many factors to consider, but regardless of whether you have decided on a career you want to pursue or are still deciding, you can begin your education at community college as an excellent, less expensive option without fully committing to a major. Community college allows you to sample a variety of class options with lower tuition costs to fulfill prerequisites before transferring to a four-year university program. It offers theoretical knowledge and lecture-style learning. They also provide more flexibility in schedules and provide support to those struggling to access higher education. Those already occupied with full or part-time work schedules, children, or other personal obligations can attend community college due to the availability of online offerings and class times outside of regular business hours.

On the other hand, if you want to land a job very quickly, trade school is also an excellent option. Like community colleges, trade schools teach you various technical skills to prepare you for the workforce but with a shorter time to complete your education. You can even complete your degree in under two years. Furthermore, trade school programs are more focused on the future career you want to pursue. Also, because trade schools are more focused on specific job skills, graduates are exceptionally well-trained in the duties required for the positions and have a better chance of being offered the jobs they choose to pursue. While trade schools are often more expensive than community colleges, they provide a better return on investment (ROI).

Attending University

While more expensive than community college and requiring a more challenging, detailed application and acceptance process, universities do provide other advanced education degrees; universities promote freedom and a chance for you to thrive while demanding you to be more independent, to move out of your current home and live in dormitories. Various chores like doing laundry and cooking will become your responsibility, helping you learn to manage your time properly.

By entering university, you will not only receive focused education in the major you've chosen but also be trained to be creative and communicative, develop teamwork skills, and many other professional attributes. These soft skills are highly valuable if you want to pursue a career. Universities are also not limited to academic activities; other extracurricular activities, like sports, music, arts and crafts, politics, and culture, will contribute to your personal growth.

The university includes a broad range of education. People all across the globe are enrolling in universities to gain expertise in the fields they're passionate about, which will give you a chance to meet people from other countries. You will be introduced to new perspectives and experiences and make friends from all around the world. University is also a great option if you want to earn a bachelor's degree or gain more advanced degrees like a master's or Ph.D. after finishing undergraduate studies if your career requires you to have a degree beyond a four-year bachelor's degree.

While universities are famous for their extravagant tuition fees, they typically offer higher amounts of financial support and scholarships than community colleges. For example, if you are a skilled sports player in high school, you can use your skills to enter a university using scholarships. Many universities offer scholarships in sports and other qualities like music performance and a high GPA. The larger the university, the more likely you may be to receive financial aid.

Going to a university is a good choice if you can commit to a full-time course load. Unlike a community college, university programs typically require you to finish your studies in four to eight years, depending on what major you pursue. Additionally, at University, you will be required to write research papers and complete other projects that teach you how to become more adept in analytical thinking.

If you're still undecided between community college or university, consider how much time and money you can devote to your education. Community college is an option if you want to enter the workforce quickly and earn a degree. If you can commit to at least four years to study and want to develop even more skills in an area that interests you, university is an option. You should also consider the type of degree or abilities required to begin the career you want to pursue.

Public vs. Private Universities

There are several differences between public and private universities, and you should review these first before choosing one over the other. Some key differences between public and private universities are listed below.

- **Tuition Cost**

    While both public and private universities provide essentially the same type of education, one of the most significant differences between them is the cost of tuition. Tuition is the primary source of funding for private universities. The state primarily funds public universities, and government subsidies cover some of the costs, so students do not have to pay full tuition. This makes public universities generally more affordable and may accept more students than private universities.

- **Program Offerings**

    Another key difference is the programs offered at public universities versus private. Many private universities tend to provide fewer academic majors than public universities. Since tuition fees are generally higher, private universities want to provide specialized education for their students. Students who are confident in their choices can benefit from this since the university focuses on fewer fields of interest. On the other hand, public universities offer more academic programs, and they tend to have larger student bodies.

- **Learning Environment**

    Public universities are larger and broader in terms of the environment. Many public universities hold classes on a massive scale, sometimes allowing non-students to attend along with enrolled students. In public universities, students must often manage their schedules and course progress, including seeking guidance from professors, counselors, or tutors. Private universities tend to have a more intimate environment with fewer students and professors who can form more personal connections, offering direct guidance to their students.

- **Reputation and Prestige**

    When students choose to attend university, they expect a quality education. Since private universities generally cost more with regard to tuition, some believe they offer better education. While most private institutions gain a higher reputation and more prestige, it's not a guarantee that they will provide a better education than public universities. However, it's proven that private universities, especially the highly-reputed ones, are still chosen by many. A study by The International Journal of Educational Management found that "the reputation of a university may affect students in decision-making" (Panda et al., 2019). Some students prefer universities with a higher reputation since they provide many advantages, such as better choices of majors, faculties, sponsorship from alumni, and renowned companies.

- **Research Opportunities**

    Students at public universities are frequently given funding and resources to complete research projects. In addition, they have more extensive facilities than private universities. Students who are serious about conducting research can take advantage of the resources provided by public universities. Private universities, on the other hand, have fewer options and funding for students to conduct their research. Though not all, most private and smaller universities generally focus their funding on institution improvements.

- **Social Life**

    Most public universities are widely known to have larger, more frequent, and lavish social events. Parties, student gatherings, and club meetings are common in public universities. While private universities can hold social events as well, they're not as large since private universities tend to have smaller student bodies. As a result, social life in a private university might be quieter and more reserved.

- **Extracurricular Activities**

    Public universities generally have various extracurricular activities, such as sports, music, arts, and other programs. They are usually managed by faculties and receive funding to encourage students to thrive outside the academic environment. Public universities have more significant events like sports championships and organize them more frequently. Although some private universities have similar extracurricular activities, the options may not be as vast as those offered at public universities.

- **Financial Aid**

    Both private and public universities offer financial aid and scholarships. However, most private institutions provide a more comprehensive range of scholarship options due to their considerable endowment funds. Statistics show that private universities can offer up to an average of a 48% discount on tuition for students (NACUBO, 2021). Public universities may offer less significant financial aid, but government funding and support will benefit students from various federal or work-study programs.

Entering the Military

Other than entering academic institutions like universities or colleges, you can choose to join the military. Enlisting in the military has its benefits. Not only will you receive an education, but you will also receive a steady paycheck, health coverage, and housing benefits. Joining the military is an excellent choice if you prefer working in a more physical environment, and it trains you to be more disciplined and organized. You can learn new skills and foreign languages and get in shape through physical training, all while serving your country. It's a hierarchical system where soldiers work their way up through the enlisted corps to officer ranks through promotion and combat training or can commission as an officer after completing a college degree.

There are things that you should consider before entering the military. Ask yourself what motivates you to join the military.

Are you passionate about serving your country? Do you wish to have a steady paycheck? Do your motivations, goals, and learning interests differ from typical academic institutions like colleges or universities? Knowing your motivations can help determine which type of military service is right for you.

I chose to go into the military to begin my higher education because I felt obligated to serve my country. The U.S. Army also provided me with income as I completed training and tuition assistance to help me achieve my four-year degree. Military training has shaped me into the person I am today. It has been a life-changing journey that has molded me into a soldier and a leader. The structure, discipline, and teamwork that I learned through training and military deployment gave me experience that allowed me to succeed later in my university education and completion of my graduate degree. I found that my experience during military service was quite challenging at first. Still, gradually I began to see the value of the education that further solidified my personal and professional skills, such as problem-solving abilities, patience, leadership, and communication. You can begin achieving your career goals through military service or turn military service into your professional career.

Military training requires a high level of physical and mental fitness. Ensure you can withstand substantial physical activity and be ready for an exhausting physical and mental routine. Before enlisting, it's preferable to seek support to help overcome this challenging transition. Contact family members, loved ones, or professionals who can encourage and support you. Military service is a significant commitment to your personal life and time; understanding the long-term commitment to military service is essential. It would be best if you also did research into the different military branches available. Taking the time to learn about the requirements, the types of training, and career opportunities can help you make an informed decision. You can do this by browsing the internet or contacting others with military experience, such as family members, friends, or recruiters.

The requirements to enlist in the military can vary, but it usually requires you to have a high school diploma or equivalent, be 17 to 35 years old, and have good physical abilities. Before entering, you should also consider your physical fitness because enlisting in military institutions usually requires you to pass physical examinations like height and weight measurements, vision and hearing tests, blood tests, and drug and alcohol tests. In addition, entering military institutions will require you to pass an Armed Services Vocational Aptitude Battery (ASVAB) test with a minimum score. The ASVAB is a series of tests used by the United States Armed Forces to assist you in identifying the Military Occupational Specialty (MOS) to which you are best suited. The test score will determine which military job or career would work best as your specialty, and each specialty has individual requirements. Below, the branches of the military you can join are listed with brief descriptions.

- **Navy**

    The Navy's primary responsibilities include protecting waterways, seas, and oceans that are not under the jurisdiction of the marine corps. It ensures marine safety by performing operations at sea, defending the nation, and giving humanitarian relief, particularly during maritime disasters. The Navy is also involved in scientific research and oceanic environmental protection, among other duties.

- **Marine Corps**

The Marine Corps is a component of the Department of the Navy that is tasked with defending advanced bases and conducting operations by land, air, and sea. The Marine Corps missions usually include direct action warfare, special operations, and humanitarian assistance.

- **Air Force**

    The Air Force is the national military branch mainly focusing on air operations and warfare. The Air Force's missions usually consist of air defense, reconnaissance, strategic bombing, and airlift. The Air Force operates various aircraft, from cargo planes to fighter jets, refueling tankers, and bombers. They also operate space-based assets such as missiles and satellites.

- **Space Force**

    The United States Space Force is a separate and distinct branch of the armed services, organized under the Air Force in a manner very similar to how the Marine Corps is organized under the Department of the Navy. The U.S. Space Force organizes and trains members to protect U.S. and allied interests in space and to provide space capabilities.

- **Army**

    The Army is a major branch of the U.S. Armed Forces. It is tasked to protect the security and defenses of the country. The Army also handles significant ground combat missions and is split into several branches, including infantry, armory, engineering, aviation, and medical corps.

- **National Guard**

    The National Guard is in charge of dealing with domestic emergencies and national security. It comprises soldiers prepared and equipped to handle various emergencies, such as major disasters, terrorist attacks, and civil unrest. In addition to reacting to emergencies, the National Guard provides community service by supporting law enforcement and participating in youth activities.

- **Coast Guard**

    The Coast Guard is military enforcement responsible for ensuring the safety and security of the nation's maritime borders. The Coast Guard operates several missions, including conducting maritime patrols, search and rescue, environmental protection, national defenses, and maritime law enforcement.

There are many similar career training opportunities between each branch of the armed forces and some career fields unique to certain military branches. If you are interested in learning more about each type of training available, you can use the following websites:

https://www.operationmilitarykids.org/military-jobs/

https://www.careersinthemilitary.com/home

The Difference Between Being Enlisted and Commissioned

The previous section discussed the requirements for general military enlistment. There is another process of joining the military through becoming a commissioned officer. Enlisted personnel generally have entered the military without a college degree. They serve in various military duties and are responsible for specific daily activities. On the other hand, commissioned officers are typically college or military academy graduates. They may make decisions regarding tactics, strategies, and special operations. The process of becoming a commissioned officer can be completed through different programs, including:

- **Reserve Officers' Training Corps (ROTC)**

    In this program, students enroll in military courses through their college or university. These courses are needed for them to obtain a degree. After graduation, students will also earn the title of Second Lieutenant and enter the military as commissioned officers.

- **Officer Candidate School (OCS)**

    The OCS prepares students for a challenging officer's life. They are trained in military culture, law, leadership skills, and physical fitness; students must have at least finished a four-year college or university degree before entering OCS training. OCS is held at Fort Benning, Georgia, and lasts 12 weeks. Graduates enter the military as commissioned officers.

- **Military and Service Academy**

    Service academies and military colleges like West Point are highly selective, but they offer fully-funded, four-year scholarships covering all learning materials, tuition, and medical coverage. Similarly, students enrolled in service academies will also be granted the title of Second Lieutenant and be commissioned officers upon graduation.

Becoming enlisted versus being commissioned in the military differ mainly in the educational requirements. Commissioned officers must finish at least a four-year study at any college or service academy and earn a degree. Additionally, a significant difference between enlisted and commissioned officers is the titles given at each level of advancement: First Lieutenant, Second Lieutenant, Captain, Major, Colonel, and General are the ranks reserved for commissioned officers. In addition, they also hold authority over enlisted service members.

Ranking for non-commissioned enlisted military personnel begins with Private, followed by Private First-Class, Corporal, or Specialist (depending on MOS). Advancing in rank beyond the initial titles requires additional evaluation and promotion into the ranks of non-commissioned officers. These ranks include Sergeant, Staff Sergeant, Sergeant First Class or Master Sergeant, Sergeant Major, Command Sergeant Major, and Major of the Army.

Military training can be a good choice if your career path or motivation cannot be met by entering academic institutions like a university or college. Joining the military can be challenging, so the best method of the approach lies in researching, understanding the required time commitment, and seeking support from others to decide whether joining the military is right for you.

Does University Prestige Matter?

We briefly discussed university prestige and reputation earlier and how the" brand" of certain universities can attract and influence some people when deciding which university to attend. Now, the question is, does it matter which university you graduated from? You might have obtained your degree from a highly regarded university, but what real advantage does it give you? We frequently assume that attending prestigious universities will provide us with a higher quality education and, as a result, better employment opportunities. However, we must carefully consider which university to attend to obtain the proper education that will allow us to advance in our careers. Choosing a university based on its reputation does not guarantee a successful future career.

In a book titled WHERE YOU GO IS NOT WHO YOU'LL BE, author Frank Bruni stated, "A prestigious school is seen as a conclusive measure of a young person's worth" (Bruni, 2017). He discussed how common claims about attending a prestigious educational institution as a guarantee to success are false; a person's worth should not be measured solely by which university accepted them. Unfortunately, many parents and students are still transfixed by educational labels. For some, obtaining a degree from well-known universities such as Harvard or Stanford will give them greater leverage in the job market, and companies will readily hire graduates from these institutions. These campuses are undoubtedly well-known for their high-quality education and successful graduates; however, they are not always the best choice for everyone.

We all have our personal needs and achievements but also our limits. When it comes to accepting students, prestigious universities are highly selective. Only some have the financial means, resources, or energy to overcome such heavy competition. I'm not saying you'll never get into Harvard or Stanford, but it would be best to consider other options that may give you a better chance of acceptance while still obtaining the same degree and level of education. Other options may even be more well-known for having a better educational program for the degree you plan to pursue.

Surveys have also revealed that it doesn't matter which university you graduated from to secure a place in a job; what's more important is your experience and knowledge. Gallup's survey of 30,000 graduates' experiences fairing in their careers added that "it's not 'where' you go to college, but 'how' you go to college." (Gallup, Inc., 2019). It doesn't matter which university you gained your degree from; some careers require a specific set of tangible skills, and an applicant that has yet to learn those skills will not be employable. This survey illustrates that you don't need to enter pricey and famous universities to make you automatically appealing to an employer. Ultimately, your skills and performance in the professional environment matter more.

Careers That Do Not Require a Four-Year Degree

So far, we have discussed educational options you can choose to prepare for your career. However, what happens if you don't prefer to go to school? If you think you need more time to commit to being a full-time student and invest your time and money to earn a degree, other options are still available. While some careers may require a college degree, many other well-paying and fulfilling jobs do not require a four-year educational commitment. Many skilled technical positions may offer excellent earning potential without a bachelor's degree. Still, other career options in the service industry offer flexibility and the opportunity to develop skills in customer service, such as hospitality and food service, without formal education. Many of the following careers require a certification which is commonly offered at trade schools and community colleges, requiring very little time and money and resulting in salaries just as high or higher than jobs that require a four-year degree. Below are some high-paying jobs that do not require a four-year education.

- **Patrol Officer**

    A patrol officer is responsible for maintaining public or traffic safety by enforcing laws within an assigned area patrol area duties of a patrol officer can vary depending on the size of the area. Still, aside from patrolling designated areas, a patrol officer will also need to respond to calls ranging from minor incidents and complaints or significant emergencies such as car accidents or crimes, arresting suspects, writing reports, testifying in court, and provide community support. The median salary of a patrol officer is $64,610 per year, ranked as the highest-paying job without a degree. Educational requirements for a patrol officer can vary. Some may only require a high school diploma. Before becoming an officer, candidates will enter a police academy, which will help them learn many practical skills, such as firearm knowledge, first aid, legal codes, and law protocols. They will also need to pass various physical exams.

- **Executive Assistant**

    The role of an executive assistant is to provide administrative support to the executive to which they are assigned. An executive assistant helps manage daily activities and responsibilities, manage schedules and appointments, organize travel arrangements, book flights, hotels, or any urgent changes, adjust and manage budgets, and supervise other support staff. The median salary of an executive assistant is about $62,060 per year. Most companies will require candidates to have a basic education and administrative or secretarial experience. This entry-level position may only require a high school diploma or an associate degree.

- **Flight Attendant**

    A flight attendant works in an airplane cabin on commercial flights. They are responsible for ensuring the safety and comfort of passengers during flights. Their duties involve greeting passengers, assisting passengers with luggage, conducting safety briefings before each flight, including how to use seat belts, oxygen masks, and life vests, offering food and beverages, monitoring cabins, responding to medical emergencies or mechanical situations, performing pre-flight and post-flight checks, and also providing customer service. A flight attendant must be skilled in customer service and communication and remain calm and professional in stressful situations. A flight attendant's median salary is about $61,640 per year and this career typically requires a high school diploma. A flight attendant must complete an airline-specific training course and pass physical examinations.

- **Sales Representative**

    A sales representative is responsible for promoting and selling products to potential customers on behalf of a company. They work in various industries, such as pharmaceuticals, fashion, beauty products, technology, and other goods. As a sales representative, one must have excellent communication skills, identify potential customers, build relationships with customers, promote and demonstrate products, and negotiate prices. A sales representative's median annual salary is about $61,600; most positions won't require formal education. This job will only require a high school diploma and experience in marketing, communication, and sometimes a foreign language.

- **Sound Engineer/Sound Technician**

    This technical profession involves producing, recording, mixing, and editing audio for various applications, such as music, films, television, and live events. A sound engineer must be proficient in operating a wide range of audio equipment, troubleshooting technical problems, collaborating with other professionals, and keeping up with technological advancements. Audio engineering can be self-learned, but many companies prefer candidates with skills certifications, specific training, or an associate degree. The median salary of a sound engineer is about $60,500 per year.

- **Electrician**

    Electricians specialize in repairing, maintaining, and installing electrical systems in buildings, houses, or other structures. The duties of an electrician include reading blueprints, schematics, or other technical diagrams, installing electrical systems, troubleshooting electrical problems, and ensuring electrical safety regulations.

    The median salary of an electrician is about $60,040 per year; they usually undergo apprenticeship programs or practical training before being hired. This job typically requires a high school diploma or a technical degree.

- **Plumber**

    Plumbers install, repair, and maintain plumbing systems in various settings, such as residential, commercial, or industrial buildings. A plumber must be able to install pipes and other plumbing components while following building codes and safety regulations. They also need to be able to read blueprints and schematics and have good customer service skills. Plumbers must have a license; earning this requires two to five years of experience, an apprenticeship, or technical education, and most will require at least a high school diploma. Safety training is also essential because injuries are common in this line of work. The median salary of a plumber is about $59,880 per year.

- **Construction Worker**

    Construction workers work in many fields, such as steelwork, bricklaying, and metalwork. They can find jobs commercially or with the government, working with materials to construct buildings. A construction worker's primary responsibilities are handling, storing, and moving material products. They need to ensure the quality of the products and operate and control many pieces of equipment, such as forklifts, jackhammers, and other equipment. Construction workers need to pass on-the-job training programs or apprenticeship programs. This job will only require a high school diploma or a technical degree. The median salary of a construction worker ranges from $53,440 to $59,340 per year.

- **Firefighter**

    A firefighter is responsible for responding to emergencies, such as fires, accidents, and natural disasters. They must react quickly to these situations and assess and control them. Aside from that, they may also need to rescue people and animals from dangerous places and provide medical assistance such as CPR and first aid at the scene of emergencies. The salary of a firefighter is $50,700 per year. Firefighter recruits must apply and complete a training course in the fire training academy. While no particular college degree is needed, firefighters need several certifications and skills, including communication skills, physical abilities, and basic life-saving skills.

- **Insurance Agent**

    An insurance agent works to sell insurance policies both to businesses and individuals. Their responsibilities are identifying potential clients needing insurance services, analyzing resources, maintaining client relationships, providing client support, and staying up-to-date with industry regulations. The median salary for insurance agents is around $49,840, and this career normally requires a high school diploma. Insurance agents must be certified or licensed, and because the industry is controlled at the state level, each state has its licensing standards. This includes passing a test or meeting specific knowledge requirements. Business experience is highly beneficial.

- **Computer Support Specialist**

A computer support specialist provides technical support and assistance to organizations or individuals. A computer support specialist should have comprehensive knowledge about network systems, computer software and hardware, operating systems, and antivirus programs since their work will involve installing and configuring them. They must also know how to diagnose and troubleshoot technical issues, formulate solutions to problems, provide technical assistance, and advise customers. To become a computer support specialist, candidates may need a skills certification or a technical degree. However, they usually rely on their technical knowledge and good customer service skills. The median salary for a computer support specialist is $49,770 per year.

- **Bus Driver**

    Besides properly operating the bus, a bus driver must follow all traffic laws, regulations, bus routes, and schedules. They also need to ensure the safety of passengers and maintain a safe, clean, and comfortable environment on the bus. Bus drivers must have a commercial driver's license (CDL), pass a drug or alcohol test, and be cleared of any conditions that could interfere with the operation of the bus. Typically, bus drivers will only need a high school diploma and be at least 18 years old. The median salary for a bus driver is $48,620 per year.

- **Real Estate Agent**

    A real estate agent helps others to buy, sell, or rent properties. They must identify potential buyers and establish good relationships with clients. Real estate agents must list properties in detail, such as creating sales, photographing, and giving tours to potential buyers. They also need to be able to negotiate sales, manage properties, and prepare contracts or other legal documents in accordance with regulations.

    The median salary for a real estate agent is $48,340 per year. To become a real estate agent, a high school diploma is adequate. Passing the state's licensing exam and completing real estate coursework are needed before being able to work under an operating license is required to work and legally ensure safe transactions between buyers and sellers.

- **Carpenter**

    Carpenters work with wood and other materials to build, install, repair, and finish structures and other surfaces. A carpenter must be able to read blueprints and other specifications to understand the design of a project. They must also have good measuring skills to cut materials accurately, using tools such as saws, drills, and chisels. The median salary of a carpenter is $48,260 per year. This job only needs a high school diploma and completion of an apprenticeship program. They must complete technical courses in blueprint reading, tool use, basic carpentry, mathematics, and safety.

You now understand the significance of planning your education before beginning a career. It is now up to you to decide which type of education is best for you based on the options available. Whether you start at a community college, trade school, public or private university, join the military, or even jump directly into a career, each can allow you to gain knowledge and experience for your professional life. While college degrees are valuable, there are some circumstances in which you may decide not to pursue higher education. A bachelor's degree is not obligatory; you can create your route to success even without a college degree. Jobs that need a high school diploma are an option, or you can seek alternative training and knowledge instead of enrolling in a university. Ultimately, obtaining a degree requires careful thinking. If you believe you will have a greater chance or satisfaction in pursuing something other than a four-year degree, alternative options exist.

If you are finding the information in the previous chapters helpful and informative, please let others know by leaving a review on Amazon for Simple Career Planning for Teens and Young Adults: A College Professor's Five-Step Guide to Finding Direction, College Admission, and Preparing for Your Dream Job.

https://amzn.to/43mVZdy

Chapter 5:

Some Roads Are Longer Than Others

Sometimes, you might find that your dream job requires higher degrees in education, such as a master's or doctoral degree. In this case, the next step after earning your bachelor's degree would be to enter graduate school. Completing a bachelor's degree is enough to set the foundations for basic knowledge in the professional scene and entry-level jobs. However, senior positions like psychologists, therapists, scientists, or college professors require you to gain at least a master's degree in your field. Graduate school gives you more specialized knowledge in a specific area. Earning advanced degrees is becoming increasingly popular today, not only for the evolving job market but also for career development. A master's degree or higher will give you more leverage in specific career fields. Although this is not always the case, master's degree holders typically have more options in many fields. Not only that, but higher degrees result in a higher salary. According to the Bureau of Labor Statistics, the median annual wage for master's degree holders in the United States was around $81,848 in 2021, compared to $69,368 for bachelor's degree holders (Helhoski & Branch, 2023).

Companies may prefer to hire people with advanced degrees because graduate education allows people to be more knowledgeable and proficient in their jobs. Furthermore, companies are aware that these individuals are dedicated learners, which would give them an advantage in the workplace. To consider investing your time and money to pursue a graduate degree, you can ask similar questions discussed in chapter three about your overall goals and objectives. Does holding a master's degree align with your career goals? Also, consider if you have the means and resources to start postgraduate education. Several other factors should also be considered, such as estimated earnings for your target career, scholarships or financial aid, and estimated student loans after you've finished your degree.

My experience in graduate school included a heavier workload than the undergraduate level. It was much more work than an undergraduate degree because undergraduate-level learning only touched the "tip of the iceberg" when it came to critical thinking and application of knowledge; graduate-level learning delved deeper into my area of focus and extended well beyond memorization of facts and basic understanding of theories. I had to read books and resources beyond the provided texts for class and wrote and presented several papers and presentations before even beginning work on my doctoral dissertation. Such a rigorous program design may lead graduate students to experience emotional fallout, such as burnout and exhaustion, but in the end, the degree is worth the effort. For me, the idea of contributing to the knowledge of my field is very fulfilling.

Your experience in graduate school may differ from mine, but generally, it will require more time commitment, and you will undoubtedly feel discouraged or intimidated by the sheer amount of effort required. However, if you can dedicate yourself to achieving a graduate degree, you will have better leverage and advantage in the job market. In this chapter, I will give you advice on pursuing graduate degrees. We will discuss what types of graduate degrees there are, what benefits they can provide you, and what careers usually require graduate degrees.

Advancing to Graduate Degrees

Graduate degrees, also known as postgraduate or advanced degrees, are academic qualifications pursued after completing an undergraduate degree (bachelor's). Universities and other higher educational institutions offer these degrees and typically require more academic effort, research, and subject specialization than undergraduate programs. Graduate programs may offer three different degrees: a master's degree, a philosophical doctoral degree, and a professional doctoral degree. These degrees will allow you to specialize and further your knowledge in specific fields related to your career field.

Master's degrees are typically designed to be finished in two years which provides advanced knowledge in a particular field and usually requires a final project or thesis at the end of study. A Doctor of Philosophy, or Ph.D., is an advanced research-based degree requiring completion and defense of original scientific work. The candidate must discover and present evidence supporting a finding in their field that was not formerly known—expanding the knowledge of the area. On average, a Ph.D. takes seven years to complete at universities in the United States. Professional doctoral degrees are specialized graduate programs that must be completed to work in certain professions, such as medical doctors, pharmacists, dentists, physical therapists, or veterinarians. The years required to complete a professional doctoral degree vary based on the profession.

I feel that this is an important place in the discussion of university education to point out that not only the type of university you choose is important, but also the major you choose for your undergraduate degree. Many high school and college students that I have met with have career goals that will require the completion of a graduate degree. It is possible, however, that after four years of college education, your desires or life's surprises may require a change of direction that leads you away from graduate school for some period of time. It is important to ensure that the undergraduate degree you have chosen is not only related to your overall career goals but also provides the relevant skills to obtain entry employment after completion of a bachelor's degree alone.

Graduate degrees offer many benefits, from greater knowledge and enhanced job prospects to better earning potential. However, pursuing a graduate degree can also be challenging. In many cases, students must be prepared to commit themselves as full-time students until the end of their studies. In this section, we will look at each type of graduate degree, what they typically offer in the program, graduation requirements, and the benefits they can give in specific job fields.

Three Types of Graduate Degrees

Because some careers may require graduate degrees, pursuing graduate education may be necessary. For example, suppose you want to get a job as a university professor. In that case, a master's degree is needed, while most medical fields, such as dentists, physicians, or psychiatrists, need a professional doctoral degree. First, let's discuss the differences between each type of degree.

- **Master's Degree**

    Pursuing a master's degree means students will gain more in-depth knowledge in their chosen field. Depending on the program in which they are enrolled, a master's degree usually takes two years of full-time study. To graduate, students must work and submit a research paper or thesis. This graduate level of education differs from a bachelor's degree because a master's program requires students to apply the knowledge acquired from their undergraduate education. This means they are expected to do far more than memorize theories from textbooks; they must be ready to create, advance, theorize, and use critical thinking to apply to their study. Students will also be doing more collaborative work with other students and researchers to complete projects. Graduate students must also get mentorship from higher-level faculty members, senior students, or other professionals in their target careers.

- **Doctor of Philosophy (Ph.D.)**

    This is another popular graduate program that leads to the highest degree in specific fields such as psychology, engineering, technology, humanities, social sciences, and medical research. This level of study is heavily research-based. Students must test their theories and hypotheses while conducting original research in their chosen field. A Ph.D. degree takes much longer to complete than other graduate degrees since students are expected to conduct original research that will significantly contribute to a body of knowledge. Furthermore, teaching or research assistantships require a considerable amount of work. Students are expected to teach at least one class per semester in addition to their other graduate student obligations. As well as writing and defending a dissertation, students must pass a comprehensive examination (also known as "comps"). Students traditionally prepare for an academic research career or a career in industry research and development as they advance toward graduation.

- **Professional Doctorate**

    Ph.D. and professional doctoral degrees will both earn the title of "doctor," but there are some differences between the two. Ph.D. programs emphasize producing original scientific research and evaluating students' findings within a theoretical framework. In professional doctoral programs, students are trained to apply the existing knowledge of their field in practical situations and solve real-world problems in their area of expertise. While they are both doctoral degrees with equal levels of education, it is essential to note that the typical careers and educational goals for Ph.D. and professional doctorates are different. Unlike a Ph.D. program, which focuses on research and discovery in a field, a professional doctorate program focuses on practice and field-related studies. The educational content of a professional doctorate focuses primarily on licensure testing required for practice in the field, for example, acquiring a medical license to treat patients or a license to practice law. There is a combination degree available for obtaining both a professional and philosophical (Ph.D.) doctoral degree in the field of medicine. The M.D., Ph.D. degree allows graduate students to obtain a license as a medical doctor as well as a Ph.D. obtained through medical research.

With the information I have provided above, I hope you have gained more insight into whether or not a graduate degree will be one of your career goals or which graduate degree would be best for you to pursue. Now let's discuss which careers usually require a graduate degree.

Careers That Require Graduate Degrees

Some careers traditionally requiring graduate degrees are listed below. Graduate degrees provide additional knowledge while opening doors for career growth and opportunity in the following fields:

Master's Degree Careers

- **Computer Scientist**

    Computer scientists work to solve problems in computing. They specialize in programming languages, software design, and other related areas. Depending on the field of focus, a computer scientist can also develop or improve the next great hardware or software machines for Google, NASA, Intel, and others. Computer scientists are crucial, especially nowadays, when everything is increasingly digital. They can develop new computing technologies and create new tools or systems to improve people's lives. They enable machine efficiency and create new communication methods by developing new networking systems.

- **Anthropologist**

    Anthropologists study the history of humans, including sociology, culture, language, and civilizations development, among other things. Anthropologists work in various fields, such as analyzing data in laboratories or collecting samples providing information about the history of human civilizations. Anthropology is an essential field of work in terms of cultural studies. It helps us understand the diversity of humans, including their customs, beliefs, and traditions. These differences will always exist in any human civilization, and anthropologists study these to help promote cultural awareness, which applies to other fields such as healthcare, business, and education. Anthropologists can also help preserve cultural heritage and maintain documentation showing valuable ancient knowledge.

- **School or Career Counselor**

    Counselors can work in different fields, such as schools, universities, or businesses. They can provide academic counseling to help students set academic goals, plan schedules, and overcome academic challenges such as learning difficulties or test anxiety. Additionally, they provide social or emotional counseling and career counseling and help students to overcome academic, professional, or personal issues to achieve desired career goals. School and career counselors are needed in almost every field of work. They can be a valuable asset because they help employees or students assess personal problems that may hinder their ability to learn or advance in a career. A counselor requires emotional fortitude and the ability to develop unique solutions to address the client's problems.

- **Psychologist**

    Psychologists are medical professionals who study human behavior and mental processes to treat various issues related to mental health. They work to assess clients' emotional, psychological, or behavioral problems, provide emotional therapy, give a proper diagnosis, and help patients find suitable remedies. Psychologists can work in private practices or healthcare facilities. Psychologists are highly valuable in the job market, just like in any healthcare field. People will always need a mental health professional to help them overcome mental health issues such as depression, anxiety, and addiction and to help them increase their overall well-being so that people can be more aware of their psychological needs.

- **Mathematician**

    Mathematicians specialize in mathematics, including mathematical theories, applications, and computational methods. They work in business, science, or engineering to solve complex mathematical theories and concepts. Mathematics is the fundamental knowledge of every other branch of science and technology, such as physics, economics, computer science, and engineering. Being a mathematician involves problem-solving, critical thinking, and logical reasoning. These skills are highly valuable in data analysis, finance, business development, and mechanical engineering, among others. Mathematics is also an essential subject in education, allowing mathematicians to also work at educational institutions.

- **Political Scientists**

    Political scientists study political systems, institutions, and political trends. They work as analysts, researching political, economic, and social movements. They can also work in organizations or companies concerned with government policies, public policies, and political groups. Political scientists can also work as teachers in universities or high schools. Understanding political systems is vital for government officials to make the most suitable decisions about governing citizens and addressing societal issues. They are also valuable for policymakers, helping to analyze complex global problems such as poverty, population decline, climate change, or terrorism and assisting in educating citizens about political systems.

- **Occupational Therapist**

    Occupational therapists help injured or disabled patients to better perform everyday activities. They plan specialized treatments and exercises for patients. Occupational therapists will assess and evaluate patients to determine their physical, cognitive, or emotional abilities and limitations and develop treatment plans based on their needs. In addition, they will also educate the patient's family members or caregivers on how to accommodate the patient's needs. Occupational therapists often work in hospitals or private home care. They are valuable in improving patients' daily lives and enhancing the healthcare system by increasing patients' independence and reducing their reliance on the healthcare system. As occupational therapists address a wide range of conditions, from severe injuries to disabilities, and mental disorders, these skills make them highly valuable in any healthcare team.

- **Survey Researcher**

Survey researchers conduct surveys to test new ideas and gather attitudes and opinions about different topics. They will collect these responses, analyze the data, and summarize them. Survey researchers are helpful in various areas, such as marketing, politics, and the economy. Being a survey researcher is essential because they help companies make informed decisions based on accurate field-reviewed data. They also help businesses and other organizations improve by conducting field research, public surveys, and gathering customer feedback to identify areas needing attention.

- **Educational Administrator**

    Educational administrators manage schools, colleges, universities, and their academic programs to ensure smooth progress for both students and educators. In addition, they will also develop and design rules, learning opportunities, and day-to-day operations in academic institutions. Educational administrators are responsible for creating and maintaining high-quality education that involves overseeing curriculums, school regulations, teacher training, and observing student performance to help them achieve their full potential. This helps to improve the overall educational environment and create a positive school culture.

- **Epidemiologist**

    Epidemiologists work in public health care to research and identify diseases among populations. They plan and manage healthcare programs and spread awareness of health issues to the public to prevent and handle the spread of community-acquired diseases. Epidemiologists usually work in laboratories and offices, specializing in various areas such as chronic illnesses, infectious diseases, environmental health, and mental health. Epidemiologists play a crucial role in understanding and controlling the spread of disease. They also help to improve overall public health in society by researching to understand the causes of disease outbreaks. Their expertise is needed to develop new treatments and prevention and inform policymakers about what must be done for the public.

Ph.D. Careers

- **College or University Professor**

    Positions as professors with graduate degrees are valued by higher institutions in every discipline, from language to science to technology. Professors are the ones who teach students, so they will need comprehensive knowledge and a wider range of expertise in a particular field before being able to instruct. While community colleges often employ professors with a master's degree, universities may require a Ph.D. Many areas taught at universities include research in a specific field. Therefore, professors will teach seated courses, conduct research, and serve as mentors for undergraduate and graduate research students. College and university professors are responsible for advancing knowledge in various fields. They not only educate students but will also need to inspire future generations by helping them to develop the knowledge, skills, and thinking abilities required to lead a successful life and make meaningful contributions to their field.

- **Computer Engineer**

    Computer engineering is fundamentally similar to computer science, but engineers generally focus on constructing machines, such as computers, laptops, and workstations. They can also create computer-based devices in today's technology, such as cars, telephones, airplanes, appliances, etc. Being a computer engineer is essential, especially in the era of rapid technological advancement. They enhance technological innovation to create new means of communication and connectivity and improve quality of life by developing assistive tools and devices for individuals with physical disabilities or other health conditions, helping them to live more comfortably. They can also contribute to economic growth since they may develop technologies and tools that many other job fields can adapt, creating new industries and job opportunities.

- **System Engineer**

    System engineers specialize in studying and understanding the complex process of engineered mechanical systems in computers and many other machines, such as those used in manufacturing. They are experts in designing, analyzing, and managing systems, from hardware and software to the physical machine that ties them together. They can figure out what's wrong with a system and develop solutions to fix it, sometimes figuring out a solution from scratch. System engineers make sure that mechanical systems work properly and effectively. They optimize system performance to help implement new and growing technologies into newer, more developed systems.

These skills are important, especially in any field that uses technology.

- **Statistician**

    Statisticians work in applying professional statistical methods to resolve real-world problems. They use statistical methods to analyze patterns and extract meaningful insights from research studies or surveys. Statisticians have been rising in demand because of statistics' importance in businesses. Some industries need to makeover their companies through data-driven decisions. Statisticians are valuable in various fields, such as healthcare, government, and environmental science.

- **Biological, Medical, or Molecular Sciences**

    Those with a Ph.D. in biological, medical, or molecular sciences research the cells of many living organisms. Individuals who focus on human research and medicine typically have a degree in pharmacology, molecular biology, cell biology, or medical laboratory science rather than general biology. This is an area in which many pursue the option of earning a medical doctorate and a Doctor of Philosophy (M.D., Ph.D.), allowing for research studies using pharmaceuticals to cure serious diseases. They can explore everything from the origins of a living organism to creating a cure or remedy for illnesses, genetic testing to diagnose and treat inherited diseases, and much more.

- **Healthcare Administrator**

Healthcare administrators or managers oversee the daily operations of healthcare facilities, including hospitals, clinics, and nursing homes. They manage staff, provide leadership, plan or implement healthcare plans or implement healthcare policies and procedures, and ensure regulations in the complex healthcare environment. A healthcare administrator will ensure that the operations of public healthcare run smoothly. Healthcare administrators are essential in creating and ensuring high-quality medical treatment for patients, managing their resources properly, and maintaining the reputations of their medical operations. They are essential for the growth and success of all healthcare industries and, ultimately, for the health of all individuals.

Professional Doctorate Careers

- **Linguist**

    Linguists are experts specializing in analyzing and evaluating different aspects of language. Some may focus on the history of languages, in-depth research, or specialize in certain language concepts, like syntax and psycholinguistics. Linguists can also work in businesses as editors, writers, or proofreaders to ensure correct grammatical and sentence structures. Linguistics is a broad branch of knowledge; it studies languages in-depth to improve communication, linguistic knowledge, and language culture. Linguists can help advance understanding in areas, such as psychology, neuroscience, or anthropology, through language acquisition and processing. They can also work to solve language-related problems in various areas such as education, business, or government by developing tools or techniques that can facilitate communication across other languages.

- **Chiropractor**

    Chiropractors are licensed professionals who focus on treating patients through manual techniques. Chiropractors will apply controlled pressure to manipulate, adjust, or restore the positions of certain joints, such as in the spine, neck, arms, and legs. They help to restore function and mobility for patients that have experienced accidents leading to damaged or misaligned joints. Chiropractors are highly valuable because they specialize in diagnosing and treating injuries to joints or muscles, particularly in the spinal area. They use non-invasive techniques such as adjustments or massage therapy, which are highly beneficial for patients who cannot be treated with surgery or medications.

- **Lawyer**

    A lawyer, or an attorney, practices law by representing clients in court. In a trial court, lawyers introduce evidence, interrogate witnesses, and argue questions of law and facts. Besides working in court trials, lawyers can also provide legal advice without needing to come into court. They can specialize in various fields, such as corporate law, criminal law, and environmental law. Demand for lawyers is rising due to their exceptional abilities in interpreting and applying the law to protect an individual's or an organization's rights. They ensure the legal process of a trial by helping clients to navigate through the complex systems of legal proceedings.

- **Veterinarian**

    Veterinarians study the medical science of animals. They apply this medical knowledge to treat illnesses or wounds in animals. Usually, veterinarians work in animal pet health care, specifically handling domestic animals like dogs, cats, or birds. Veterinarians can also work in zoos with exotic animals and in farming or racing industries with large animals such as cows and horses. Veterinarians are essential in treating animal diseases. This is an exceptional skill to protect animals' rights, ensure the health of domesticated animals, and help them live healthy lives. Veterinarians are also needed to preserve nature and protect endangered animals.

- **Surgeon**

    Surgeons work to perform operations on patients, such as removing, cleaning, or replacing damaged internal organs. The surgeon can perform various tasks in many practices, such as cardiothoracic surgeons, who specialize in surgeries in the chest area, addressing conditions of the heart and lungs. Neurosurgeons perform operations on nervous systems, particularly in spinal cords or the brain, while the plastic surgeon performs operations to alter, restore, or reconstruct patients' physical appearance. Aside from performing surgical procedures, surgeons are also responsible for assessing, managing, and monitoring a patient's preoperative and postoperative periods and prescribing medications.

- **Pharmacist**

Pharmacists are licensed professionals who fill prescriptions for medication written by medical doctors to ensure that the medication is appropriate and the dosage is correct for patients. They also advise patients on dosage, instructions for taking drugs, and any side effects that can occur. Pharmacists work in hospitals, animal clinics, the military, and retail pharmacy companies. Pharmacists are essential in educating patients about the safe and effective use of medications. They are needed to prevent medication errors, abuse, and other medication misconduct by providing patients with important information.

- **Neurologist**

    Neurologists assess patients' neural disorders, particularly disorders connected with the brain, spinal cord, nerves, and muscles. Neurology is a focused study of the nervous system, which coordinates body activities. They address illnesses such as stroke, epilepsy, and others. Since the nervous system regulates all body movements and functions, neurologists work with healthcare professionals throughout the healthcare system. They must ensure that a patient's complex neurological condition is treated correctly and develop a comprehensive treatment plan.

- **Dentist**

    Dentists are professionals who properly diagnose and treat problems surrounding teeth, gums, and the oral cavity. They provide dental examinations, cleaning, and sometimes surgical procedures if needed. Dentists can work in private or governmental institutions. Oral health is closely related to general health. Dentists are also trained in diagnosing more serious medical conditions that may manifest inside the oral cavity, such as diabetes, throat or oral cancer, or autoimmune diseases. Since dentists can detect these conditions early, they can help prevent more serious illnesses from developing.

Benefits of Getting Graduate Degrees

A graduate degree can give you many benefits. Gaining a graduate degree means you are an expert in a particular field; this gives you an advantage in the job market since hiring companies prefer candidates with advanced skills and knowledge, especially for management positions. Here are some key benefits you can gain by completing a graduate degree:

More Career Opportunities

People who earn graduate degrees can qualify for a broader range of positions. Moreover, they will be eligible for senior and leadership roles and gain an advantage in career advancement. Companies would prefer to hire these individuals for senior positions.

- **Networking Opportunities**

    Studying in graduate programs can provide more opportunities to connect with other professionals, especially in a specific area of study. In graduate programs, networking in both academia and industry are essential since graduate students aren't only expected to study but also gather and contribute their knowledge in the field.

- **Improves Personal Growth**

    Graduate programs encourage students to work on personal development. While graduate students are expected to conduct an original research project, they are also expected to apply these findings in the real world. This teaches critical thinking and encourages creativity, independence, and innovation.

- **The Ability to Change Careers**

    Holding a graduate degree can also assist people in changing career paths. Because of their increased range of job opportunities, those with a graduate degree can simplify the process of changing careers. Advanced knowledge and skills are highly valuable in the job market, allowing someone to transition from an industry position to an academic position, for example.

- **Potential Increase in Salary**

    A survey by the BUREAU OF LABOR STATISTICS found that graduate students have an average of 25% salary increase (Torpey, 2018) after completing the advanced degree. People with graduate degrees are also more likely to be hired in higher positions, potentially increasing their earnings.

In summary, getting a graduate degree, such as a master's, Ph.D., or professional doctorate, will need more effort than a bachelor's degree. A graduate degree involves hard work, dedication, perseverance, and focus. Still, such degrees can give you more leverage in the job market, such as increased salary, job security, and career opportunities. They can enable you to enter senior or higher positions, giving you more impact and influence in a career in which you are passionate.

Chapter 6:

The College Starting Line

So far, you have learned about many options for career and education. While some jobs require only one or two years of formal training or education, others may require a four-year bachelor's degree, master's degree, professional doctorate, or even a Ph.D. Whether you plan on earning a trade certification, a technical career degree from community college, a four-year undergraduate degree, or continuing to graduate school, similar processes must be completed to start your journey toward career success. Choosing the right institution to attend, filling out applications, and paying for classes may require significant effort. Through this process, many questions may arise, such as:

- How do I choose the right school for my education?

- How can I distinguish myself from the thousands of other applicants?

- What qualities do admissions officers seek in a new student?

Despite the anxiety and uncertainties often accompanying your college admissions, it is also a time for growth and self-discovery. Like other teens and young adults, you are experiencing a significant change in your life, being forced to confront your strengths and weaknesses, identify your passions, and envision your long-term goals. You are also expected to be independent and take risks to get what you want. At this stage, guidance is crucial in helping you grow as a person, as this can be very overwhelming if you aren't getting the advice you need. Although the process can be complex, it can be navigated successfully. You can ease your way through college admissions with the right guide and careful preparations. You will be on your way to pursuing higher education in no time, opening the door to so many opportunities in the future and aiding you in advancing your career.

In this chapter, I will outline the general process of applying for a higher education program and gaining financial support to obtain the knowledge and training you need to succeed. The following will include some of the essential tips you need to know: how to manage time and money throughout the process, how to apply to colleges or universities, how to gain information and work through scholarship applications, and navigating the process of obtaining financial aid.

College Preparation and Application

Knowing where to start in applying for a college can be challenging. Even after choosing which school you would like to attend, additional tasks include writing an entry essay, submitting test scores, and many other requirements. Fortunately, many resources and guides are available, including high school counselors, college advisors, and online resources that can provide direction and support. Additionally, you can attend college fairs or visit certain schools to gain more information about their programs and campus cultures.

Choosing schools that match your goals and interests is one of the most important aspects of starting college. Consider available programs, eligibility requirements, campus size, location, and extracurricular activities that interest you. It may also be wise to focus on the school's reputation and accreditation to consider how it fits your academic and personal ambitions. Once the list of potential schools is compiled, the next step is to begin the application process. This often involves gathering personal data, transcripts, test scores, and other materials. It is also best to devote significant time to crafting essays showcasing your unique skills, abilities, and experiences if an essay is one of the requirements for application to the institutions to which you are applying.

The road to college is long and winding but also full of possibilities and opportunities. With the proper support and dedication, applying for college can be a transformative experience that sets the stage for a successful future. In this chapter, we will discuss each of the important steps in applying to and preparing for your college experience.

Applying for College

Initially, applying to college might seem intimidating, but preparing for what you must submit beforehand will be a significant step toward your future. Completing college applications may be stressful to some people, but successful completion of the process and receipt of acceptance letters come with a great sense of satisfaction and achievement.

The good news is that most colleges and universities follow the same standard application process. You can begin by following these steps:

Get Informed

It is best to become familiar with the general information on each institution's website to which you plan to apply. Visit the campus or attend college fairs where they provide information and answer questions. This will help you to become familiar with the college, find out what program interests you the most, and identify whether or not the school will align with your academic and personal goals. Some of the critical things you need to know include:

- The kinds of programs, majors, and extracurricular activities offered.

- The documents you should prepare before applying to the college.

- Deadlines for application submissions.

- The campus culture, rules, terms, and conditions.

- Available financial aid or scholarship programs.

Most academic institutions now provide online information on their campus websites, making it easier to access answers to your questions. If you'd like, you can also contact the college advisors and ask for private counseling.

Gather the Necessary Materials

Prepare the necessary documents to begin applying to colleges. This includes your personal information, such as your social security number or ID number, address, etc. Other documents you might need to prepare include the following:

- Application forms–schools will require you to complete basic personal information on a specific form.

- Academic transcripts–grade reports from high school or other academic institutions you've attended.

- Letters of recommendation–letters from trusted adults that can describe your abilities.

- Personal statements–create a short essay about yourself, your talents and skills, and your academic and career plans.

- Exams–if the institution you're applying to needs you to take an entrance exam, be sure to collect the appropriate information for scheduling and completing the exam.

- Financial information–some schools may require you to give information about your or your family's income and tax returns to see if you are eligible for scholarships and financial aid.

Organize Materials

You must organize the documents you need to apply for college—personal records, school-related transcripts, and forms, and create to-do lists. The idea is not to feel overwhelmed by the number of documents you must submit and fill out throughout the process. You can remain organized by following these steps:

- Create physical or virtual folders to store important documents.

- Create a checklist to track your progress through each application process. An example checklist is below:

  1. Gather personal information, including social security number, mother's maiden name, and personal or family tax statements (W2s).
  2. Write a personal essay if the college or university requests one.
  3. Get three letters of recommendation from teachers, coaches, or other authority figures that can highlight your strengths (academic achievement, leadership, dedication, etc.).
  4. Find out how to request official transcripts from your current or former school (high school and college).

- Build a spreadsheet to stay up to date with submission deadlines.

- Fill out the college application and attach the required documents (you will likely be filling out an application at more than one institution if you plan to attend a four-year university).

- Pay the application fee (plan ahead for which applications are most important to you so that you can ensure funds are available for these applications first).

- Fill out a FAFSA Application (this will be covered in the financial aid section below).

Following these steps will help you be more efficient in managing your time and applying to the colleges you are most interested in attending.

Personal Statement Essays

This is a general requirement to enter most universities and even some competitive community college programs. They will encourage you to demonstrate some of your unique traits, talents, or skills that will set you apart from other applicants. This will allow you to express yourself beyond your grades and test scores. Aside from your GPA and an overview of your academic experience, you can include anything that reflects your personality. For example, if you are skilled at musical instruments and have participated in numerous recitals. Maybe you are a black belt in karate or volunteer through your local church or community center. This increases your chances of being noticed during the admissions process because you have a skill that can help you thrive outside of the school environment. In essays, it is important to be thorough, set aside time to brainstorm ideas, create an outline, and write drafts. Then, you can ask for feedback from your friends, family members, teachers, or counselors to construct a final draft.

Asking for a Letter of Recommendation

It is advisable to ask teachers for letters of recommendation several months before the application deadline. Teachers and academic counselors will be overwhelmed with recommendation letter requests near the end of the school year, so allow plenty of time for them to prepare the letter and gather the relevant data from you. Teachers and academic counselors might also need information about your skills, grade scores, or even a draft of your statements to identify the strengths they want to highlight in a recommendation letter.

Reviewing and Submission

Double-check and review all documents that you plan to submit. Ensure the information is correct and free from typos or misspellings. While some institutions will allow you to submit application documents online, some will require you to submit them in person or through a specific mailing process. Read the application instructions carefully and identify the process for each individual application.

Applying for Scholarships

Due to rising tuition fees for education, scholarships can be an option for you to save money and help ease the financial burden of a college education. Today, scholarships are widely available at individual institutions and through state and national organizations. You can earn scholarships by being skilled in a sport, or a craft, being proficient in a foreign language, or showcasing other unique talents. The opportunities for a scholarship are endless. Once you're awarded a scholarship, the money will usually go directly toward your tuition, and you are not required to pay back the scholarship money. Let's start by getting to know how you can find and apply for scholarships.

- **Finding Eligible Scholarships**

    The first thing you need to do is find resources describing specific scholarships. Many scholarship programs provide information through online websites, advertisements, mobile applications, and other means. You can also learn more about scholarship programs at the college or school you plan to attend. Both public and private universities offer many scholarship programs. Simply Googling "Scholarships for _____ majors" and entering the college major you want to pursue can give you a large amount of information and options for scholarships.

Certain scholarships will be available to all students, while others will be awarded based on specific characteristics or merits (GPA, test scores, sports, skills, etc.). Some scholarships are considered departmental scholarships. For example, only students majoring in social sciences, psychology, or law may be eligible. Generally, the more specific the eligibility rules, the less competition you will have and the higher your chances of being awarded the scholarship.

You should also extensively research available scholarship programs to find the one that best fits your abilities, needs, goals, and eligibility criteria. Need-based scholarship programs are based on your family's capacity to pay for tuition, whereas merit-based scholarships are based on your achievements; they may be more restricted to topics such as arts, music, athletics, or academics. However, additional situation-based scholarships are available for minorities, marginalized communities, people with disabilities, or people from developing countries.

It also is essential to search for specific scholarships based on your intended major or study, those provided by your college or university, by the state, and national scholarships. If you still want more guidance, you can talk with an academic counselor, teacher, or instructor to help you find the perfect scholarship program.

- **Understand the Scholarship Requirements**

    After you have listed the scholarships to which you want to apply, you should also understand what needs to be done to proceed with the application process. Pay attention to the requirements, necessary documents or materials, and essay requirements. Some scholarships will ask you to write an essay similar to the personal statement you used for college applications. You may be provided with a specific topic to write about. However, this time make sure you align everything with the targeted scholarship and provide reasons why you should be awarded the scholarship. In addition, some scholarship programs will ask you to submit letters of recommendation, copies of test scores, grades, and GPA reports. Creating a resume can also be one of the necessary steps. This trains you to address yourself professionally and encourages you to showcase your academic qualities in a more formal manner.

    It's easy to lose track of your progress, mainly if you apply to multiple scholarship programs. To prevent this, creating a spreadsheet and calendar is a good idea to remind yourself of the dates, submission deadlines, and award announcement timelines. The process of applying can be time-consuming, especially when you need to compose new essays and gather letters of recommendation. Some scholarships require you to make a video statement or prepare for a performance. You will be busy during this process, especially if you're already attending school and are occupied with classes and homework or working full-time and caring for a family. Make sure to schedule everything in advance and keep up with deadlines.

- **Check the Status of Your Submission**

  After you have successfully submitted all the necessary documents and completed the application process, the only thing left to do is to wait for the results. You will also need to check the status occasionally; sometimes, it will take weeks or months to be notified of scholarship awards.

Obtaining Financial Aid

Financial aid is an additional funding program usually provided by the government, academic institutions, or private organizations to help students pay for their education. Tuition prices can be a barrier for people considering higher education, so providing financial resources for students can also benefit institutions because more students will consider enrolling in their institution. These programs can assist students in reaching their full potential and goals.

To receive financial aid, you must complete the Free Application for Federal Student Aid (FAFSA). The FAFSA form can help you qualify for several types of financial assistance. The US Department of Education supplies this form, and grants are usually need-based. Several financial aid sources include Pell Grants, Federal Supplemental Educational Opportunity Grants, and Teacher Education Assistance for College and Higher Education (TEACH) Grants. These resources can help students reduce some student loans, textbook expenses, or other expenses needed to pursue education. Federal student loans are loans that need to be paid back after graduation but at a lower interest rate than personal private loans obtained from banks. These loans are based on your academic year, grades, and tax status. Financial aid options are available to make education more affordable for all. In this section, I will discuss some of the financial aid programs available and what you need to apply for financial aid. Additional sources of financial aid are described below.

- **Aid for International Study (Study Abroad Programs)**

    If you want to study or get a degree at a school outside of your home country, you can apply for federal financial help. The kind of funding you can receive and the process by which to apply will differ based on the aid program. Your student status, program of study, and country of residence will all impact your eligibility. If you meet the eligibility requirements, you may receive financial aid for a semester or a year of study abroad. Before receiving federal student aid for study-abroad programs, you must complete the FAFSA application. Contact the financial aid staff at your school to learn more about submitting FAFSA forms.

    To earn a degree from an overseas school, you must determine which international institutions participate in federal student aid programs. Here are some tips to help you prepare for studying abroad and receiving federal student aid:

    o Plan in advance. The process usually takes a few weeks to a month, so plan for this process.

    o Do research. If you're interested in one particular school, check their website and determine whether they support federal student aid and the supported programs. Ask yourself the following questions:

- Does the international institution offer the degree you want?

- What are the enrollment policies, costs, and resources you should prepare for as an international student?

  o Keep track of your paperwork. Passports and visas, medical insurance, emergency contacts, and housing forms. Living abroad can be complicated without the necessary paperwork to avoid problems in another country.

  o Note the names or contact information of financial aid officers. Get their email address or phone numbers in case you have any questions throughout the process.

- **Aid for Military Students**

  There is available funding from the federal government or private institutions for veterans, future military recruits, active duty personnel, or family members of veterans or active duty personnel. Suppose you or a family member is a part of the military or are pursuing a military career. In that case, you can be eligible for student aid to help pay for educational expenses. There are several military financial aid programs, including:

  - **Army and Air Force ROTC.** There are several scholarship programs available. The ICSP or In-College Scholarship Program is an example, and you may be eligible to enter even if you're already in

121

college. Some programs target students pursuing certain technical degrees or foreign languages, although students from varying majors are also eligible. Whether you're a freshman or a sophomore student, the program awards scholarships based on merit. You can learn more about Army and Air Force ROTC programs by visiting the following websites:

https://www.goarmy.com/careers-and-jobs/find-your-path/army-officers/rotc.html

https://www.afrotc.com/scholarships/college/types/

- **Navy ROTC.** Scholarship and financial aid programs are offered for a partial or full four-year military program. You can also earn scholarships for approved Navy ROTC colleges or universities. Learn more about the programs offered through the following website:

  https://www.navy.com/start

- **The GI Bill.** The GI Bill provides help for military service members transitioning to civilian life. It is also one of the most popular programs for funding college and higher education for military members. To be eligible for the GI Bill, you must have served at least 90 days on active duty or 30 days if you were discharged due to a service-related condition. In most cases, recipients of the GI Bill have completed or are currently contracted to serve as active-duty military members or reservists.

- **Military Student Loan Assistance Programs.** The Air Force, Navy, Army, Marines, and National Guard offer loan repayment for active duty service members with existing student loans. In addition, they also offer repayment assistance to eliminate student debt. These programs are available to military members who have served in military deployments and members with service-related injuries.

- **Aid from Colleges or Universities**

    Financial aid is also available from your specific college or university after enrolling in a program at the institution. Some universities or colleges offer larger financial aid packages than others, and the type of institution funding may depend on tuition rates. Generally, the higher the tuition rate, such as in private universities, the larger the financial aid award. You can visit your school's financial aid office and ask the department whether they have financial aid programs for students in your major.

- **Personal Loans**

    Borrowing money directly from a bank is another alternative for covering the cost of college tuition. A loan is a sum of money that you must repay with interest. The terms and conditions of your loan will be individualized, and you may be required to repay the loan after the academic year, per semester, or after you have completed your degree. You must be aware of your repayment options to repay the loan effectively. It should be noted that the interest rates on personal loans may be significantly higher than that of federal education loans. Additionally, current government student loan forgiveness packages do not apply to private student loans, making them, in my opinion, a "last resort" for covering college tuition.

- **Work-Study Programs**

    Work-study programs at schools allow you to earn money by working part-time. These programs will help you make money to pay for tuition and other educational expenses and give you valuable work experience that can benefit you in your future career. Work-study programs typically require you to work off-campus, on-campus, at public agencies, or non-profit organizations. Your salary in this type of program will be the current federal minimum wage. The total work-study award will also be determined by the type of work you complete, the skills required, the type of financial help you need, and the budget level of your institution.

Based on the tips and resources I have listed and described above, I hope you have a more comprehensive knowledge of applying for scholarships and other educational assistance. There are unlimited opportunities for you to pursue higher education without worrying about being unable to afford them. Academic institutions are becoming more supportive in encouraging people to complete their education and providing financial support for students toward a successful future.

Chapter 7:

Changing Course and Reaching the Finish Line

For some, deciding on a college major can be difficult. Before now, you may have believed that the major to which you have dedicated your entire academic life was best for you, but what happens when you realize that your chosen major no longer fits your goals and interests? The decision to change majors can be difficult, especially if you have invested much money, time, and effort working on your current major. Moreover, changing your path after starting college courses can lead to falling behind in completing individual classes, adjusting to a new academic environment, and potentially delaying graduation. You may incur additional costs, but changing majors may be necessary in some circumstances. Reasons you might feel like you may need to change college majors may include losing interest in your current major, feeling like you don't possess the necessary skills to keep pursuing your current major, or you might have recently changed your mind about your career goals for the future. Nonetheless, making a change is a significant process that shapes the course of your professional career and academic life.

When deciding to change college majors, you must recognize the factors that may cause you to decide on a change. Evaluate whether changing majors can offer you benefits that will allow you to pursue your passions and reach your full potential. Your career goals should also be considered. If you believe your current major will not help you achieve the skills and knowledge required for your desired profession, it may be time to change majors. Make sure to revisit and reevaluate your list of long-term goals before deciding to leave one area of study for another. This chapter will discuss changing direction in college and what typically happens when you do so. You may have finished a college degree already or only a few courses in another field, but you a curious about what would happen if you shifted your intended career after starting college. I will also discuss some of the possibilities after graduating from college to assist you in making decisions about your next steps.

The Many Paths You Can Take

Did you know that according to research, around 75% of students have changed their major at least once in their college career? (Sun, 2022). This shows just how flexible the education system can be. Students can change courses halfway to accommodate their needs in education more fully. You can use this opportunity to try out a different major that interests you and ensure you make the right choice for your future. Remember that changing your college major is not a result of poor judgment. You might regret wasting time and resources when you could have made a better decision.

Changing majors is okay; it signifies your development and self-discovery. By identifying and deciding what's necessary for your future, you are shaping your path to success. Switching majors indicates that you have become more in touch with your career goals. Attending college and university is, after all, a process for developing oneself. There's room for improvement, both academically and personally. Some people might need more time to determine their right path. I encourage students willing to extinguish their passion for learning something entirely new to go through the process of switching majors and view it as an avenue toward a fulfilling career future.

What to Consider When Changing Your College Major

Changing majors will require some time and preparation. While switching majors can be done with ease, this may only sometimes be the case. It can be a complicated process depending on what institution you're currently enrolled in, what major you're currently studying, and to what major you plan to switch. So, it would be best to adequately prepare before switching majors. Here are some things you should consider before deciding to change your college major:

- **Time and Money**

    We all agree that pursuing higher education will take considerable time and money. Changing majors may involve completing extra semesters or credits to graduate. Having a financial plan before you switch majors is crucial. Consider strategies such as securing scholarships or financial aid, as described in the previous chapter, as this will help you finish your degree successfully. Furthermore, you should think about your graduation date. Because changing degrees typically require taking more classes, your graduation date may change. Are you willing to continue your education for another year or semester? For example, switching from music to culinary arts requires more time. Switching between similarly related fields and capabilities, on the other hand, will be easier, for example, going from biology to medical laboratory.

- **Consult with an Academic Counselor**

    An academic advisor or counselor will help you find a good choice. You will be encouraged to switch to a specific major that aligns better with your personality or academic performance. Academic advisors are specially trained to handle situations where students want to change majors and can provide you with all the options available. They will also help you to consider various advantages and disadvantages when switching majors and explain the process of changing majors to help you achieve your goals.

- **Decide Early**

    Changing majors within the first or second year of a four-year degree is preferred since you usually complete most of the general education courses required by all degrees and have yet to invest as much time in courses specifically required for your declared major. If you switch majors later, you may have already taken degree-specific classes that will not count toward your new degree.

- **Identify the Benefits of Switching**

Switching majors can be beneficial for the right reasons. You should change majors if it can benefit your professional and academic life later. Changing to a new degree path may be the right decision if you're falling behind in class or feel like your subjects are no longer attractive. Don't switch majors, however, just because you dislike a professor or if you're only a few credits away from graduating.

Each college major may have drawbacks, such as mismatched learning styles, certain classmates you dislike, or one or two courses you're not as interested in. It might be an unwise choice if you decide to switch majors to avoid these types of discomforts in your studies. Every program will have some aspect that is less appealing. If you're experiencing these issues, you can seek assistance from an academic counselor. They may ask you to consult with a professor or lecturer to accommodate your learning style, provide help with your assignments, etc. In any case, you should consider why you want to switch majors; changing majors may not be the best decision if it only involves minor discomfort.

Changing majors is a significant development in your academic life and should be pursued with careful research and assessment. You can consult with academic advisors, career counselors, or faculty members to ensure that you will benefit in the long run. Ultimately, the most crucial aspect of changing majors is remaining consistent with your academic, personal, and professional goals while maximizing your resources and opportunities. Whether you choose to stay with your current major or change it, the most important thing is to remain focused and motivated.

Options to Consider After Graduation

You may wonder about your choices after graduation as you progress through your academic pursuits. After graduation, you can continue your education, enter the workforce, or explore new opportunities. With many options available, you must reflect on your goals and interests to identify the best pathway forward. Common choices after graduation include looking for an entry-level job or continuing your education. However, other decisions, such as internship or volunteering, can further enhance your academic and professional experiences. Remember, you may feel slightly disoriented after graduating from college, and it's okay to feel uncertain at first. If this is the case and you have not found the "perfect" job in your current city or town, moving to a new location may increase your options. This may also be an excellent time for you to reflect on the long-term goals you had planned for yourself as you entered your college program and determine the next best move to achieve them. In this section, we will look at some of the common post-graduation options, and I will offer some guidance about making the best decision moving forward.

- **Continue Your Education**

    After graduation, you may choose to continue your education through a graduate program. This can include attending other academic institutions to get more knowledge or pursuing a higher degree like a master's degree or Ph.D. Upon graduating, you should know what you'd like to do for employment. If the job you seek requires a graduate degree, it may be best to continue your education immediately.

- **Look for a Job**

There are all kinds of jobs you can apply for after graduating. You can try part-time or full-time employment depending on whether or not you will continue your education immediately. This is a great time to showcase all your obtained skills, unleash your creativity, knowledge, and experiences gained in college, and apply them to the workforce, earning money. There are so many entry-level jobs to which fresh graduates can apply.

- **Attending Online Classes**

    Online classes are an excellent idea to help fill your time as you browse the job market and submit applications. Online lessons are excellent whether you do it for enjoyment or to gain more information on a specific topic for future employment. Online courses are known for being affordable, flexible, and accessible; some are even free. You can also attend online classes while working part-time or in an internship program. Not only is it highly beneficial, but it also increases your employability.

- **Work for Your College**

    Some colleges or universities may accept recent graduates for positions at their institutions, for example, in admissions, academic or research assistants, or academic guidance and counseling. Consider this if you love working in an educational environment, as it may also give you opportunities for other employment in higher education. Talk with your administrative staff at your school to ask if there are any suitable positions for a fresh graduate.

- **Teaching or Tutoring**

    This is a great starting job for fresh graduates. Most teaching or tutoring jobs require a bachelor's degree; some even enable you to go overseas. Many foreign countries seek young and fresh candidates to teach language in schools. This is also an excellent opportunity for new graduates to travel, experience life in other countries, and get experience in the workforce. Another alternative is being an online tutor. These days, online tutors are highly preferred by many students. A survey by Cengage revealed that about 73% of students prefer online learning, especially since the onset of the pandemic (Kelly, 2021). You can apply to be an online tutor for companies or organizations that provide online learning classes.

- **Volunteering or Internships**

    Look for volunteering or intern opportunities to build up your skills further. Often, volunteering programs will train you to develop skills such as leadership, time management, and completing everyday workplace tasks. You will also be trained to develop soft skills like communication. Some volunteering programs will also offer paid positions, which can be a great way to get direct experience in a particular field while earning some money. Internships are similar in the fact that you will be trained to develop your skills in a specific field. Most programs offer paid internships, a great experience to put on your resume to let hiring companies know your first-hand, post-degree experience in the field.

- **Move to a New Place**

Exploring new places can be beneficial whether you're moving to a new city or country. Moving closer to hiring companies and attending interviews may be necessary to take advantage of the best career opportunities. Large cities tend to have more job opportunities than small ones. If your city doesn't offer you many job opportunities, you can consider moving elsewhere. Make sure to plan accordingly by setting aside some time to research the location you're interested in moving to and look at the cost of living and housing options compared to the salaries offered for the positions you are interested in. Ask your prospective company if they will cover some expenses for relocation. Many companies will provide a relocation budget to assist you in moving to another place, preferably closer to their office.

After graduation, you have a wide range of options. You must choose your next steps while corresponding with your future goals, career ambitions, abilities, and passions. Remember that your journey after graduation is unique, whether you begin a career in your current city, relocate to explore additional career options, or continue your education. Don't be afraid to take risks and explore your options; remember that every experience can teach you something new. As you embark on this new chapter of your life, keep an open mind, be true to yourself, and discover success and fulfillment along the way.

Conclusion

Guidance can be a potent tool for empowering the next generations of professionals. In this book, I hope I have provided inspiration, practical advice, and step-by-step guidance to help you overcome obstacles in making decisions about your academic and professional futures and prepare you for successful and fulfilling careers. I wrote this career planning book to navigate the complex and rapidly changing world of the job market. I hope it has been informative, engaging, and helpful, it has provided you with an extensive overview of the career and educational landscape and tips and strategies to make the most suitable choices for your future.

In hindsight, you might have previously thought that personality tests are only for entertainment or a brief window to understand yourself better. I hope you have learned about various personality types, how they can affect you in the workforce, and how important it is to identify your personality type and interests to thrive in specific jobs or careers. Personality tests are, in fact, an essential aspect in choosing what career will fit you best. You can compare your unique personal qualities to your interests and find your dream job. Additionally, this book has illustrated the essential questions and considerations you need to think about before choosing a career, your core values and purpose, and the effort and careful preparation required. Choosing a career is essential in self-growth and discovery before committing to a profession. In the end, you will need dedication, perseverance, and consistency.

While pursuing advanced education can be complicated, you have been provided with steps for applying to colleges and universities, applying for scholarships and financial aid, and the differences between each educational option allowing you to make the best choice for your career education. All academic institutions, from community colleges to universities and military institutions, will provide different benefits in forging your path to success. The journey through academics to professional life is undoubtedly challenging. There may be small "bumps in the road", choices you wish you had made differently, or significant changes in direction that may lead you down a different path entirely. For this reason, I have also included information about what you should consider when changing direction in your career choices.

Lastly, many opportunities are available after you finish your education. Post-graduation can be confusing or even overwhelming for some. With the guidance from this book, you will be more prepared for an exciting future after graduating from college. Whether jumping directly into the workforce in your new career or taking a less traditional path through alternate employment options, the post-graduate pathways I mentioned will give you new experiences to discover and learn.

At its core, this book for teens and young adults should inspire you to pursue your passions, reach for your dreams, and help you to achieve your personal goals, but you also need to be aware of the importance of hard work, effort, and commitment. I encourage you to think creatively, take risks, embrace changes, and help develop the skills, resilience, and mindset needed to thrive in the ever-evolving job market. I hope this career planning book has been an excellent investment for your future, and thank you for dedicating your time to take this journey toward your future. I hope I have provided you with the tools and knowledge you need to navigate opportunities available in the working world and build rewarding and fulfilling careers that reflect your unique personal qualities, skills, and interests.

If you found this book helpful in planning your goals and finding a direction for your future career, please leave a review on Amazon.

https://amzn.to/43mVZdy

References

Andoi, S. (2022, September 1). *5 Factors To Consider When Choosing A Career.* Www.money254.Co.ke. https://www.money254.co.ke/post/5-factors-to-consider-when-choosing-a-career-campus-money-diaries

Armentrout, D. P., Winters-Miner, L. A., & Stout, D. W. (2015). Resiliency Study for First and Second Year Medical Residents. *Practical Predictive Analytics and Decisioning Systems for Medicine*, pp. 462–530. https://doi.org/10.1016/b978-0-12-411643-6.00023-5

Ashton, M. C. (2013). Personality Traits and the Inventories that Measure Them. *Individual Differences and Personality*, pp. 27–55. https://doi.org/10.1016/b978-0-12-416009-5.00002-5

ASVAB Career Exploration Program. (n.d.). Aswabprogram.com. https://www.asvabprogram.com/media-center-article/66

Birken, E. G. (2022, September 28). *Return On Investment (ROI).* Forbes Advisor. https://www.forbes.com/advisor/investing/roi-return-on-investment/

Birt, J. (2023, March 16). *16 Options To Consider for What To Do After College.* Indeed Career Guide.

https://www.indeed.com/career-advice/finding-a-job/what-to-do-after-college

Bloom, J. J., Halasz, H. M., & Sizemore, D. (2012). Making Change Work: Empowering Students Who Are Changing Majors. *The Mentor: Innovative Scholarship on Academic Advising, 14*. https://doi.org/10.26209/mj1461300

Boogaard, K. (2023, January 18). *The Pomodoro Technique Really Works, Says This Productivity-Hack Skeptic*. The Muse. https://www.themuse.com/advice/take-it-from-someone-who-hates-productivity-hacksthe-pomodoro-technique-actually-works

Bouchrika, I. (2022, September 26). *Does it Matter Where You Go to College? It Depends on Who You Are*. Research.com. https://research.com/universities-colleges/does-it-matter-where-you-go-to-college

Bouchrika, I. (2023, January 23). *Difference Between Public & Private University: Tips Which One to Choose in 2023*. research.com. https://research.com/universities-colleges/public-private-university-difference

Bruni, F. (2016). *Where You Go Is Not Who You'll Be: An Antidote to the College Admissions Mania* (Updated,Expanded). Grand Central Publishing.

Bureau of Labor Statistics. (2022, September 8). *Employment Projections - 2021-2031*. http://Www.Bls.Gov/Emp.

CareerAddict Team. (2022, December 23). *Should I Go to University? A List of Pros and Cons*. CareerAddict. https://www.careeraddict.com/should-i-go-to-university

Careers That Require a PhD or Doctoral Degree. (2022, October 24). Graduate School. https://gradschool.louisiana.edu/blog/careers-require-phd-or-doctoral-degree

Carlton, G. (2023, March 23). *Should You Change Your Major? | BestColleges.* BestColleges.com. https://www.bestcolleges.com/blog/should-you-change-your-major/

Center, C. K. Y. (2022, October 26). *Know the 5 Major Personality Traits and the Corresponding Career Choices.* Kentucky Counseling Center. https://kentuckycounselingcenter.com/know-the-5-factor-personality-traits-and-career-choices/

Chamorro-Premuzic, T. (2015, July 6). *Ace the Assessment.* Harvard Business Review. https://hbr.org/2015/07/ace-the-assessment

Cherry, K. (2023, March 11). *What Are the Big 5 Personality Traits?* Verywell Mind. https://www.verywellmind.com/the-big-five-personality-dimensions-2795422#citation-1

College Applications: How to Beting – BigFuture. (n.d.). Bigfuture.collegeboard.org. https://bigfuture.collegeboard.org/plan-for-college/your-college-application/get-organized/college-applications-how-to-begin

Community College vs. University | Pros & Cons. (2023, January 31). Mount Wachusett Community College. https://mwcc.edu/blog/community-college-vs-university/

Compton, R. J. (2003). The Interface Between Emotion and Attention: A Review of Evidence from Psychology and Neuroscience. *Behavioral and Cognitive Neuroscience Reviews, 2*(2), 115–129. https://doi.org/10.1177/1534582303002002003

Computer Engineering Frequently Asked Questions. (n.d.). UH Department of Electrical and Computer Engineering. https://www.ee.uh.edu/undergraduate/computer-engineering-faq#:~:text=In%20other%20words%2C%20computer%20engineers,and%20many%2C%20many%20other%20products.

Cooks-Campbell, A. (2021, May 13). *How to have a good work-life balance (hint: it's not just about time). Www.betterup.com.* https://www.betterup.com/blog/how-to-have-good-work-life-balance

Coursera. (2022, May 4). *How Long Does It Take to Get a PhD?* Coursera. https://www.coursera.org/articles/how-long-does-it-take-to-get-a-phd

Dev App Academy. (2022, December 12). T*he 5 Best Jobs for Someone With Type A Personality.* The Cohort by App Academy. https://blog.appacademy.io/best-jobs-type-a-personality/

Drexel University School of Education. (n.d.). *The 10 Benefits of Online Learning in a Virtual Classroom.* School of Education. https://drexel.edu/soe/resources/student-teaching/advice/benefits-of-online-and-virtual-learning/

Epps, T. (2020, December 1). *Private vs. Public Colleges: What's the Difference? | BestColleges.* BestColleges.com.

https://www.bestcolleges.com/blog/private-vs-public-colleges/

Federal Student Aid. (n.d.). Studentaid.gov. https://studentaid.gov/understand-aid/types#aid-for-international-study

Forsey, C. (2022, October 3). *How to Discover Your Long-term Career Goals, According to Experts.* Blog.hubspot.com. https://blog.hubspot.com/marketing/the-next-step-career-quiz

Gallup, Inc. (2019, December 30). *The 2014 Gallup-Purdue Index Report.* Gallup.com. https://www.gallup.com/services/176768/2014-gallup-purdue-index-report.aspx

Hanson, M. (2022, January 21). *Average Cost of Community College.* Education Data Initiative. https://educationdata.org/average-cost-of-community-college

Hargrave, M. (2022, December 27). *Is University Prestige Really That Important?* Investopedia. https://www.investopedia.com/articles/personal-finance/051915/university-prestige-really-important.asp

Hartnett, H. (2022, April 8). *3 Personality Tests and How You Can Use Them in the Workplace.* Fast Company. https://www.fastcompany.com/90738776/these-3-personality-tests-still-have-value-in-the-workplace

Helhoski, A., & Branch, T. (2023, February 17). *Is a Master's Degree Worth It?* Nerd Wallet. https://www.nerdwallet.com/article/loans/student-loans/is-a-masters-degree-worth-it#:~:text=You%20could%20earn%20more%20with,h olders%20who%20earned%20about%20%2469%2C368.

Herrity, J. (2022, October 27). *8 Personality Tests Used in Psychology (And by Employers)*. Indeed Career Guide. https://www.indeed.com/career-advice/career-development/types-of-personality-test

James, G. (2019, October 23). *What Goal-Setting Does to Your Brain and Why It's Spectacularly Effective*. inc.com. https://www.inc.com/geoffrey-james/what-goal-setting-does-to-your-brain-why-its-spectacularly-effective.html

Kelly, R. (2021, May 13). *73 Percent of Students Prefer Some Courses Be Fully Online Post-Pandemic*. Campus Technology. https://campustechnology.com/articles/2021/05/13/73-percent-of-students-prefer-some-courses-be-fully-online-post-pandemic.aspx

Khalfani-Cox, L. (2021, May 10). *Why Most Employers Don't Care Where You Went to School*. The Money Coach. https://askthemoneycoach.com/employers-dont-care-went-school/

Latham, A. (2022, October 31). *The Return on Investment for Trade Schools Vs. Bootcamps*. SuperMoney. https://www.supermoney.com/return-investment-trade-schools-versus-bootcamps/

Ma, J., Pender, M., & Welch, M. (2019). *Education Pays 2019 THE BENEFITS OF HIGHER EDUCATION FOR INDIVIDUALS AND SOCIETY*. research.collegeboard.org. https://research.collegeboard.org/media/pdf/education-pays-2019-full-report.pdf

Mailhot, B. (2022, July 1). *How To Find and Apply For Scholarships for College*. Going Merry. https://www.goingmerry.com/blog/how-to-find-apply-for-scholarships/

Mcleod, S., PhD. (2023, February 13). *Type A and Type B Personality Theory—simply* Psychology. https://www.simplypsychology.org/personality-a.html

Mendis, D. (2022, December 19). *Want to Change Your Major? Here's What You Should Know*. Shorelight.com. https://shorelight.com/student-stories/want-to-change-your-major-heres-what-you-should-know/

NACUBO. (2021, May 19). *Private College Tuition Discounting Continued Upward Trend During COVID-19 Pandemic*. Www.nacubo.org. https://www.nacubo.org/Press-Releases/2021/Private-College-Tuition-Discounting-Continued-Upward-Trend-During-COVID19-Pandemic

NERIS Analytics Limited. (2020, September 30). *Is There an Ideal Career for My Personality Type?* Www.16personalities.com. https://www.16personalities.com/articles/is-there-an-ideal-career-for-my-personality-type

Officer Candidate School (OCS) — Today's Military. (n.d.). Www.todaysmilitary.com. https://www.todaysmilitary.com/joining-eligibility/becoming-military-officer/officer-candidate-school

Panda, S., Pandey, S. C., Bennett, A., & Tian, X. (2019). University brand image as competitive advantage: a two-country study. *International Journal of Educational*

Management, *33*(2), 234–251. https://doi.org/10.1108/ijem-12-2017-0374

Patterson, R. (2022, May 21). *What to Do After College: 9 Options to Consider*. College Info Geek. https://collegeinfogeek.com/what-to-do-after-college/

Pencavel, J. (2015). The Productivity of Working Hours. *The Economic Journal, 125*(589), 2052–2076. https://doi.org/10.1111/ecoj.12166

Personality Max. (2021, December 10). *Best Career Matches for Each Personality Type*. https://personalitymax.com/personality-types/careers/

Plumer, B. (2013, May 20). *Only 27 percent of college grads have a job related to their major*. Washington Post. https://www.washingtonpost.com/news/wonk/wp/2013/05/20/only-27-percent-of-college-grads-have-a-job-related-to-their-major/

Powell, F., Kerr, E., & Wood, S. (2022, November 3). *Understanding Financial Aid for College: A Guide*. US News & World Report. https://www.usnews.com/education/best-colleges/paying-for-college/articles/an-ultimate-guide-to-understanding-college-financial-aid

Premack, R. (2018, August 2). *17 seriously disturbing facts about your job*. Business Insider Nederland. https://www.businessinsider.nl/disturbing-facts-about-your-job-2011-2?international=true&r=US

Program Insights. (2021, August 27). *16 Jobs that Require a Master's Degree*. post.edu. https://post.edu/blog/jobs-that-require-a-masters/

Robert Glazer. (2019, August 9). *Talent vs. Skill, What's The Difference?* (#21). https://robertglazer.com/friday-forward/talent-vs-skill/

Scholarships.com. (n.d.). *Apply For Scholarships - Scholarships.com*. https://www.scholarships.com/financial-aid/college-scholarships/scholarship-application-strategies/apply-for-scholarships/

Shemmassian. (2022, August 31). *Don't Know What to Do After College? A Practical Guide to Help You Decide — Shemmassian Academic Consulting.* Shemmassian Academic Consulting. https://www.shemmassianconsulting.com/blog/i-dont-know-what-to-do-after-college

Student's Guide to Financial Aid and the FAFSA | BestColleges. (n.d.). BestColleges.com. https://www.bestcolleges.com/resources/fafsa/

Sun, K.-L. (2023, August 23). *What Does It Mean to Be Undeclared? | BestColleges.* BestColleges.com. https://www.bestcolleges.com/blog/what-does-undeclared-mean/

Surgeon job profile | Prospects.ac.uk. (n.d.). Prospects. https://www.prospects.ac.uk/job-profiles/surgeon

The Guide to Earning College Credit in High School. (2013, June 25). OEDB.org. https://oedb.org/advice/guide-to-earning-college-credit-in-high-school/

Torpey, E. (2018, August 24). *Employment outlook for graduate-level occupations : Career Outlook: U.S. Bureau of Labor Statistics.* https://www.bls.gov/careeroutlook/2018/article/graduate-degree-outlook.htm#:~:text=The%20median%20annual%20wage%20was,%2468%2C090%20for%20master's%2Dlevel%20occupations.

University of Washington. (n.d.). *What Is Graduate Education?* grad.uw.edu. https://grad.uw.edu/about-the-graduate-school/what-is-graduate-education/

USAGov. (2019). *Join the Military | USAGov.* Usa.gov. https://www.usa.gov/join-military

Walden University. (2022, October 22). *What's the Difference Between a PhD and a Professional Doctoral Degree?* Retrieved March 15, 2023, from https://www.waldenu.edu/online-doctoral-programs/resource/what-is-the-difference-between-a-phd-and-a-professional-doctoral-degree

What is a Master's Degree: Everything You Need to Know | Franklin.edu. (n.d.). https://www.franklin.edu/blog/what-is-a-masters-degree#:~:text=A%20Master's%20Degree%20is%20a,knowledge%20within%20a%20specific%20area.

Why It's Totally Okay To Change Your Major and How To Make The Switch. (2022, April 5). Niche. https://www.niche.com/blog/why-its-totally-okay-to-change-your-major/

Williams, A. (n.d.). *How Does Joining the Military Help Pay for College?* Www.edmit.me. https://www.edmit.me/blog/how-does-joining-the-military-help-pay-for-college

149